THE ROLE OF CRITICISM IN HINDUSTANI MUSIC

The Role of Criticism in Hindustani Music

PRIYA KANUNGO

KANISHKA PUBLISHERS, DISTRIBUTORS
NEW DELHI-110 002

KANISHKA PUBLISHERS, DISTRIBUTORS
4697/5-21A, Ansari Road, Daryaganj,
New Delhi-110 002
Phones : 2327 0497, 2328 8285
Fax : 011-2328 8285
E-mail : kanishka_publishing@yahoo.co.in

First Published 2006

ISBN 81-7391-838-4

PRINTED IN INDIA

Published by Madan Sachdeva for Kanishka Publishers, Distributors, 4697/5-21A, Ansari Road, Daryaganj, New Delhi-110 002, Typeset by Sunshine Graphics, Delhi, and Printed at Chaudhary Offset Process, Delhi.

Acknowledgement

I chose to work on a book entitled *A Critique on Criticism (of Music and other Performing Arts)* for two reasons. First, I have been a student of Hindustani music for several years and have an abiding interest in it. Second, I have also been a journalist for some years and have written on the arts. My book is, therefore, an attempt to bring these two personal interests of mine together.

I am grateful to Dr. Najma Parveen Ahmad for her invaluable advice and encouragement in researching and writing this book.

Above all, had it not been for the blessings of my parents, my guru, Pt. Deepak Chatterjee and, had my daughter Akanksha not been patient, this book might not have seen the light of day.

AUTHOR

Introduction

The performing arts of India go back several centuries. It would be a mammoth and probably impossible task to describe all of them here. So, for practical purposes, only some of the popularly-known forms of the three broad streams of the performing arts – music, dance theatre–have been dealt with in this book.

In an article entitled *The Tradition of the Performing Arts*, Dr. Kapila Vatsyayan has compared the performing arts of India to "the single-bodied and many-armed image of Durga or Shiva in his form as Nataraja, ever destroying, ever creating new forms of the dance *Tandava*. These symbols signify at one level the unified equilibrium, the still-centre, and at the other, the continual play of "energy" and rhythm in multiple plural forms. The two aspects are inter-connected and mutually dependent. The varied art forms, like the multiple hands and arms (of Shiva or Durga), thought distinct and separate, are all limbs of the same body."

No wonder, Bharata's *Natya Shastra,* which most consider the fountainhead of the performing arts, gives equal weight to music, dance and theatre. After all, each of them is a combination of the three put together.

Yet, it is difficult to speak of one tradition of communication through the arts, particularly the performing arts in India. In fact, there are traditions of performing arts, each with layers of complexities and often, borrowing from each other. In spite of these complexities, and the apparent picture of an eternal timelessness which is repetitive, a close look reveals that each of these classical forms can be clearly identified both in terms of the evolution of artistic form and style in time and its socio-cultural milieu in space.

This book begins by giving a short description of some of the prime classical performing arts of the country in the first chapter. Since the focus is on Hindustani music, the second chapter goes back in time to record some of the fundamental concepts of Hindustani music like raag and rasa, what well-known musicologists down the centuries have said as to what should be considered "good" music and then, what changes have occurred over time – whether they are structural and grammatical changes in Hindustani music or situational and dictated by time, economics, style and technology.

In many ways, the introduction of the microphone and the facility to record music had far-reaching effects on both practitioners and connoisseurs of music. For practitioners, this meant not having to strain their vocal chords to reach the farthest end of the auditorium, as also those with weak voices getting a chance to be "heard". Recorded music meant not having to travel miles to listen to your favourite musician, but the luxury of sitting at home and experiencing that pleasure--not once but as many times as you choose. It also meant that music students can record a lesson and keep listening to it when needed instead of going over the same lesson with the guru several times. Being exposed to only one *gharana* as a student has since, not been a necessity. These, and many more modern trends have made a difference to the face of Hindustani music over the years.

Chapter three is, perhaps, the core of the book. This is where the subject of music criticism is addressed. Some critics when interviewed, said they don't have much space now in newspapers to write reviews. It is a fact that most publications don't entertain articles on the performing arts today–neither for projecting issues concerning the art world nor reviews of performances. The explanation given is that people aren't interested in the classical arts any more; that popular arts like Indipop, rock and jazz concerts are the crowd pullers. Therefore, most publishing houses (with the exception of *The Hindu* perhaps) believe that if people aren't getting attracted to the classical performing arts, they certainly won't be interested in reading about them in newspapers and magazines. At the most what we see today is curtain raisers and announcements of such programmes. Of course if there is a celebrity (who that particular journalist/photographer considers a "celebrity", read, you might have a bit thrown in about how "spectacular", "exquisite" or "fantastic" the performance was.

About writing a knowledgeable yet critical review, some critics said that if a negative statement has been written about a performance, there have been instances where the performer has lashed back by saying: "You can't sing/dance. Who are you to say anything negative about the performance?" It is true that what a critic writes about a star performer does not really affect his/her performers. But it is of great importance when it involves an upcoming artiste. It is a kind of publicity–good or bad – but it is publicity nevertheless and getting "known" is important for a performing artiste.

The book also looks at the calibre of critics in the country today. Many of the veterans had learnt music at some point in their lives. Somewhere along the way they might have realized they could be well-informed listeners rather than performers. That's when they might have become critics.

Then there are some among the critics who can't recognize common raags. They are the ones who, among the group of writers in that particular newspaper/magazine, might have professed an interest in music and were therefore sent on the assignment of reviewing a concert. There are others too, who write long, flowery pieces, without touching upon a single technical aspect of the concert. You might wonder whether the article is a demonstration of the poetic acumen of the critic or an apology of a review. Many times it is a combination of the two, with the former dominating.

The issue of patronage can't be far away from criticism of performing arts. The question whether patrons of Hindustani music understand it critically needs to be answered. In India, the biggest patron of music and dance is the government. A bunch of officials, with a few "experts" thrown in, form various committees. They pick and choose the deserving artistes. It is important to note that on many of these occasions, the expert might be suggesting that artiste A or B should be given a chance not merely on the basis of merit. So, many times, the patron is the benefactor not because he/she has any critical knowledge of music.

Then there are the corporates who patronize art. Some of them even run well-managed *gurukuls* like the Sangeet Research Academy in Kolkata, which is funded and managed by ITC. However, most business houses lend their support from outside, by sponsoring a festival or an event. In such events, it is the star musicians who attract the crowds and some promising artistes are given warm-up acts, that is, they start the evening's recital and after that performance, a Pt. Jasraj, Pt. Bhimsen Joshi or Smt. Kishori Amonkar takes center stage.

During the process of compiling information about this book, it was observed that the '80s were, perhaps, the best time for classical music performances. That's when both the government and the corporate sector extended their largesse to Hidustani classical music. Some believe that the star performers who benefited greatly at this time didn't really "package" themselves well, because of which audience interest in Hindustani music declined. Others feel it is the arrival of Indipop that proved comparatively more attractive and, therefore, took audiences away from classical music in the '90s.

The fourth chapter of the book looks at issues concerning classical dance and theatre. Theatre bears the burden of being probably the most difficult to sustain – the involvement of a large number of people who need to rehearse for many weeks, costs involved, finding a common time, sets, and the lack of sponsors. On top of that, it is usually anti-establishment. The advent of supper theatre (largely English theatre) lent a certain glitziness, but this kind of five-star environment, with dinner thrown in as part of the ticket charges couldn't sustain itself for long. We are now back to risqué musicals in English, National School of Drama (NSD) productions and the once-in-a-while interesting, independent plays.

Dance on the other hand is flourishing, both in terms of the number of dancers increasing each year and, possibly, the number of opportunities to perform also increasing proportionately. But again, the space for dance criticism in publications is miniscule. And being a dance critic is a tall order. You have to know the intricacies of each of the dance forms, be it Bharat Natyam, Odissi, Kuchipudi etc. and follow the languages used so as to understand the songs that are sung as accompaniment to the dance. Conversely, it would be difficult to find a Bharat Natyam critic or an Odissi critic. There has also been an effort in the book to trace the role of music in both dance and theatre over the decades.

The role of criticism in the performing arts is not restricted to just newspapers and magazines. An attempt has been made to see how it is represented on television, in universities and among intellectuals in seminars.

The apex government body for the performing arts, the Sangeet Natak Akademi, is supposed to look for new talent, support dying art forms and hold seminars to address problems in these areas, apart from holding regular festivals. In fact, it is this body's critical analysis that can make the maximum difference to any performing art or artiste. Unfortunately, the accusations against the Akademi far outweigh what they are credited for.

When interviewed, most artistes agreed that constructive criticism has helped them on many occasions to see what they had overlooked. It was a good means for them to correct their flaws. But at other times, they felt that it was often meaningless and was said for the sake of saying something.

It is for those who read or see (on TV) such criticism, perhaps, a useful medium for comparing notes and checking whether their opinions (as the audience) tally with that of the critic (who is considered "informed" and knowledgeable in the field) and also for gathering more information on the subject.

More on the subject, when you read the book...

AUTHOR

Contents

1

The Performing Arts

Introduction

The performing arts of India go back several centuries. It would be a mammoth and probably impossible task to describe all of them here. So, for practical purposes, only some of the popularly known forms of the three broad streams of the performing arts–music, dance theatre–have been dealt with in this book.

In an article entitled *The Tradition of the Performing Arts*, Dr. Kapila Vatsyayan has compared the performing arts of India to "the single-bodied and many-armed image of Durga or Shiva in his form as Nataraja, ever destroying, ever creating new forms of the dance *Tandava*. These symbols signify at one level the unified equilibrium, the still-centre, and at the other, the continual play of "energy" and rhythm in multiple plural forms. The two aspects are inter-connected and mutually dependent. The varied art forms, like the multiple hands and arms (of Shiva or Durga), thought distinct and separate, are all limbs of the same body."[1]

No wonder, Bharata's *Natya Shastra*, which most consider the fountainhead of the performing arts, gives equal weight to music, dance and theatre. After all, each of them is a combination of the three performing arts.

A short description of some of these prime classical performing arts of the country follows:

INDIAN CLASSICAL MUSIC

When one talks of Indian classical music, there are two kinds that the country recognizes–Hindustani and Carnatic.

Both these music streams trace their origin back to the Vedas and are based on the twin concepts of *raga* and *tala*. Both emphasis on the use of *gamakas* as an aesthetic imperative, but at the same time, there is much that separates the two forms.

In terms of geography, the music heard in the southern states of Tamil Nadu, Andhra, Karnataka and Kerala is Carnatic and that in India's north, east and west is Hindustani. In metropolitan areas like Mumbai, Delhi and in a place like Dharwad, both styles thrive side by side.

Doing a comparative analysis between the two musical streams, Shakuntala Narasimhan, in her book *Invitation to Indian Music* says: "In general, a composition in Tamil or Telugu can be identified as Carnatic and those with lyrics in Hindi, Bengali or Urdu would be Hindustani. But obviously language on its own cannot categorise a piece of music as Carnatic or Hindustani. For one thing, Sanskrit lyrics can be found in both styles and there are examples of Marathi lyrics set to music in the Carnatic idiom. Besides, instrumental music that uses no language can still be identified clearly as Hindustani or Carnatic. Even in vocal renderings, an *alapana* or tune without words can be recognized as north or south Indian. This is because of the differences in the kinds of *gamakas* used in each style–certain varieties like the *meend (jaru), andola* and *leena* are typically Hindustani and certain others like the *kampita, sphurita* and *nokku* give a musical phrase a typically Carnatic flavour. This, however, does not mean that one type of *gamaka* is exclusively Carnatic and another Hindustani. All *gamakas* are employed in both, but certain varieties predominate in one and certain others in the other.

Apart from the differences in the compositions performed in the two styles–the *kriti, javali, padam* and *tillana* in Carnatic music and the *khayal, thumri, dadra* and *tarana* in the Hindustani system–the south Indian style seems, from the point of view of the lyrics, more wordy and devotional in content than the north Indian style which seems to have far fewer words with the accent on melodic content rather than word content.

Carnatic music also seems more rhythm dominated perhaps because of the emphasis on *kriti*, which is the mainstay of concert repertoire. In contrast, the *khayal* as it is sung today, has a loosely knit, pliable line of lyrics that individual performers mould and stretch according to their fancy, with the *sam* as the only rhythmic constraint.

One major difference between the two styles that strikes laymen as well as connoisseurs is that Carnatic music concert adopts the fast-to-slow sequence in items while the Hindustani format reverses this sequence. These two sequences in Hindustani and Carnatic music are dictated by the characteristics of the *gamakas* emphasized in each–the chromatic nuances are such that they carry better and are more effective in medium tempo in the south Indian style and vice versa for the north Indian style."[2]

The other point of difference is that in Hindustani music, the speed is increased gradually while in the Carnatic system, it is strictly in geometric progression. Whether it is *sargam*, singing or other improvisations, there can be no intermediate speeds in Carnatic music items. In Hindustani music, the tabla is a must for clocking the *tala* cycle, whereas the Carnatic musician can make do by marking time with his/her hands.

Shaakuntala Narasimhan adds: "Hindustani recitals usually offer two (or more) compositions in the same *raga* (the *vilambit* and *drut*). This would never happen in the Carnatic style. A south Indian concert could feature more than one percussionist –the ghatam and/or kanjira often provides rhythmic accompaniment along with the mridangam. In contrast, the tabla is the sole accompaniment for rhythm in north Indian recitals.

There are *ragas* that are common to both styles, some of them go by the same name too in both systems while others use the same notes but are known by different names.

Hindustani *ragas* like Brindavani Sarang, Jaijaivanti, Des have been incorporated into Carnatic music. Similarly, the Hamsadhwani scale of Carnatic music is now a popular Hindustani *raga*.

There is one major difference though in terms of incorporating *ragas* of one stream into the other. The idea of a melodic *swaroopa* (entity) as distinct from the definition of a scale in terms of the notes taken, finds greater acceptance in Hindustani music than in Carnatic. For example, Deshkar and Bhoop are identical in terms of scales. But Deshkar is a morning *raga*, emphasizing the upper tetrachord and the other is a night-time melody, stressing on the lower notes."

Whatever the points of difference, the height of musical excellence in both styles lies in *raga* improvisation. Artistry and skill is judged by how well the improvisation is planned, how fertile in terms of imaginative combination of notes and how evocative the delivery is, besides the level of intricacies displayed.

INDIAN CLASSICAL DANCE

There are several dance forms in India. However, there are only a handful of them that have got recognized as "classical". Each of those that come under the ambit of Indian classical dance has a distinct form, tempo, language, music and dress. Today they are part and parcel of the art world and have their own connoisseurs. Given below are some of them:

Bharat Natyam

Bharat Natyam, perhaps the most well-documented dance form of South India, is said to have been brought to its present form more than a 100 years ago by four eminent dance masters and musicians of Tanjore–the four brothers, Ponniah and Sivanandam, dance masters of Sri Brihadiswara Temple and the royal court at Tanjore; and Chinniah and Vadivelu, court musicians and composers.

The dance repertoire was so arranged that the various styles of dance composition could be presented in a single evening's performance as entertainment, according to the taste of the last few kings of Tanjore.

In its pure form, *Nritta* in Bharat Natyam interprets the language of rhythm and melody in diverse patterns of curves, angles and lateral movements. Precise rhythmic movements of the hands and continuous footwork form the crux of the dance.

Adavu is the basic unit of dance composition. It is the cadence of hands combined with rhythmic movement of the feet and harmonious flexion of the body in precise co-ordination. *Adavus* form the basic vocabulary of dance composition and must be perfected by the pupil right from the beginning. A series of *adavus* strung together in a *tala avartan* (section of timing) forms a dance pattern. While the feet articulate the rhythm, formalized gestures of the hands and arms combined with stylized movements of the body form the basis of this dance.

Describing the paces that some of the dance forms go through, Ragini Devi says in her book *Dance Dialects of India* : "The characteristic stance in Bharat Natyam is the deep knee bend or *plie*. The *plie* requires that the distance between the bent knees should equal the distance from the nose to the naval. Flexion of the knees is an essential part of the dance.

This dance form has three tempos–slow (*vilambit*), medium (*madhya*), and quick (*drut*). The slow tempo is doubled for medium and quadrupled for quick timing. All three timings are essential for contrast and rhythmic variety.

The characteristic embellishments of this dance further add too its beauty. Embellishments like the rhythmic gliding movement of the neck synchronized with eye movement, the flexion of the breast turned to the side with the head inclined and eyes directed to the shoulder need to be performed with finesse.

This classical dance also has an evolved musical back up The *nattuvanar* is the chief musician and conductor of the dance. He sings the melody, recites the rhythm patterns and simultaneously plays the complex rhythms on the cymbals in consonance with the drum (mridangam). The voice, flute, veena and violin carry the melody. And, just as the western musician plays the score of a great composer without alteration, so the dancer performs the *nattuvanar's* composition.

Normally, a dance recital goes through the following format:

Alarippu is the ritual dance prelude accompanied by rhythmic syllables intoned by the *nattuvanar* and accompanied by the drum in slow, medium and fast tempo.

In the second dance, *Jatiswaram*, patterns of melody are given visible form in the varied sequences of the dance.

This is followed by *Sabda*–which is a gesture song. It is a song in praise of the deity or king. The first verse (*pallavi*) is sung with rhythmic syllables (*sabdas*) and danced as a prelude, refrain and finale.

Next comes *Varna*. It is the most elaborate composition in the repertoire and calls forth the versatility of the danseuse in pure dance and mime. The music is completely *raga* based and a sequence of pure dance follows the end of each verse. The fascinating element of *Varna* is the exposition of the transient moods of love (*sanchari bhava*) in mimetic dance. This portion of the recital reaches its climax in intricate dance patterns which are danced to the melody sung with scale notes and repeated with gestures and dance that interpret words.

After *Varna*, there are gesture songs once again in which the danseuse takes on the role of a devotee or divine heroine.

Tillana is the grand finale of the recital. It is pure dance and perhaps the most graceful and lyrical. The words of the song consist of simple rhythm syllables continuously repeated by the singer."[3]

The dance costume and jewellery has also evolved with time. The traditional costume of the Devadasis used to be a tight bodice or *choli* and the gold embroidered draped sari, a silk cloth of nine yards. When the art of the Devadasis emerged as Bharat Natyam, a new style of costume was created for the dance. The sari was cut and shaped into draped pajamas with a fan-like pleated piece in front and a separate piece around the hips. This costume has become fashionable as it is easy to change between items. It is also considered modest as it covers most of the body. However, some dancers still prefer the more artistically draped sari tied in a particular fashion.

Manipuri

It is believed that the history of Manipur Raas, the mystic dance of Krishna, Radha and the *gopis*, goes back in time more than 200 years to a dream of a ruling prince, Karta Maharaj. Legend says that he was driven out of Manipur by a *usurper* and took refuge with the Raja of Assam. Karta Maharaj was asked to prove his prowess by a feat of strength with a wild elephant. He had a dream in which Lord Krishna appeared to him and told him to hold a rosary of sacred *tulsi* beads when approaching the elephant. After conquering the animal, he was to make an image of Krishna from the wood of the jackfruit tree obtained from the Kaina mountain and install it in a temple in Manipur. The prince did as directed and conquered the elephant. With the help of the Raja of Assam, he led an army to Manipur and reconquered his kingdom. The temple was built in Imphal and the image of Krishna installed. Lord Krishna then appeared to Karta Maharaj in a vision and revealed his mystic ' Raas dance.

Karta Maharaj, who was a poet and lover of arts, directed Guru Swarupanand to seek the collaboration of all the great masters of dance in Manipur and adapt the older dance form of Manipur–the *Jagoi-Nin-Thoag-Pareng* (translated as dances by the king of dancers, Lord Siva) to the Raas Leelas of Lord Krishna. This recreated dance form was called 'Nat-sankeirtan' or dance with *kirtan* (devotional songs of the Vaishnava poets in praise of Krishna).[4]

The Raas is the epitome of grace. One pose seems to merge into another and gestures have a softness and the pervading mood is serene and dreamlike. There are no beguiling glances and amorous gestures. The costume for this dance form is also strangely blissful. The skirt of green for Radha and red for the *gopis* is richly decorated with sequins and mirrors and stands out stiffly at the hem. The skirt swings in a fascinating manner in the dance and puffs out when the dancer squats. This dress is however quite unlike what women in Manipur normally wear (a wide cloth wrapped around the body under the armpits). It is usually a girl who takes the role of Krishna in the Raas Leelas. She wears an elaborate headdress with an ornamental peacock feather crest, a jacket, yellow dhoti and decorative garlands.

Cymbal, drum and flute usually play along with the *kirtan* while the dance is in progress. The rhythms of the dance are played on the Pung or mridanga. A dancer first has to learn the rhythm syllables of the *talas* as played on the drum before she is able to dance correctly. The feet are not lifted and their movements are hardly visible beneath the skirt. In fact, there is no display of footwork as in other forms of Indian classical dance. The knees are kept close together and bend sideways in the dance poses (*bhangis*). There is a simultaneous deflection of the waist also. Over all, Manipuri dance is based on four basic dance movements that recur in all Raas dances and are called Chali or Chari.

These dance festivals are performed on full-moon nights and each Raas Leela is a different love episode of Krishna and Radha. It is believed that only when the illustrious poet Rabindranath Tagore discovered this dance form and introduced it to his students in Shantiniketan that Manipuri grew in popularity beyond the State. Today, it is a well-recognised classical dance form and is performed all over the world.

Kathak

The origin of Kathak is traced in ancient literature to the storytellers, the Kathakas, who recited *kathas* or stories from sacred Puranas and epics with gestures and dance. Kathak as a classical dance form was a religious art performed in the royal *durbars* of the Rajasthan state in medieval India.

The oldest known Kathak dancer was Bhanuji, a devotee of Siva and an expert in Siva Tandava. His disciples and descendants made their home in Jaipur and their style of dance came to be known as the Jaipur gharana of Kathak dance.

Around the 16th century, there was a revival of Vaishnavism in North India. The blossoming of dance, music, poetry and painting was inspired by devotion to Krishna. Surdas, the well-known Vaishnava poet-composer sang of the love of Krishna, Radha and the *gopis* and the songs became popular. The group dances of the Rasadharis of Brindavan and Mathura, the Raas Mandala and Raas Leelas, were a refined folk form of Radha-Krishna dances accompanied by *kirtanas*. The gestures, whirling movements and pauses, and the group of rhythm syllables in the texts of the *kirtanas* are primary folk elements that developed a more elaborate classical form in Kathak dance.

Akbar, who was the Mughal ruler during this period, was a great patron of Hindu music and dance. The Kathak gurus and dancing girls came into prominence because of him. But the Mughal rulers didn't particularly care for the Radha-Krishna legends and mythological themes of Kathak dance. The religious aspects of Kathak and its traditional music were, therefore, discarded in court dances.

Music and dance received lavish patronage from the *nawabs* of Avadh in the 18th and 19th centuries. Among these *nawabs*, Wajid Ali Shah was a true connoisseur and an accomplished musician and Kathak dancer himself. He is believed to have originated the *Thumri* style of music and composed lyrical love songs based on classical music. These songs were sung by Kathak dancers and interpreted in expressive mime. The meaning of a single poetic phrase was expressed in different ways with *mimetic* gestures and facial expression.

Kathak dance owes much to Wajid Ali Shah who encouraged his court dancers to develop the expressional aspect of Kathak within the tradition. Their style of Kathak is called the Lucknow *gharana*. Binda Din and Kalka Prasad are some of the foremost exponents of this style of Kathak. The descendants of Kalka Prasad–Shambu Maharaj, Lacchu Maharaj and Birju Maharaj–are exponents of the Lucknow *gharana* at present.

The Janki Prasad *gharana* of Benaras.

The Janki Prasad *gharana* is another branch of the Jaipur style of Kathak that flourishes in Benaras. This style is noted for grace and precision and uses dance syllables exclusively for its rhythm patterns. Drum syllables are never used as in other schools of Kathak. Janki Prasad and his descendants propagated this style of Kathak and even to this day it flourishes.[5]

Pure Dance in Kathak

Footwork is the distinctive characteristic of Kathak. The beauty of Kathak dance is the perfectly harmonized fluid patterns of the arms and curves of the body that give visible expression to the rhythm patterns of the feet, variations in tempo, permutations of the timing cycle in cross rhythms, rapid turning movements and sudden still poses are the technical formulae of Kathak. Flow of movement, grace and poise are its aesthetic qualities.

As footwork is the basic element of Kathak, strings of bells, at least one hundred for each foot are tied around the ankles to mark the rhythm patterns of the feet. The slap of the feet on the floor can be distinctly heard. Drums provide the accompaniment–the pakhawaj or the tabla. A simple tune continuously repeated is played on the sarangi to mark the time cycle.

A Kathak performance begins with the time-honoured Ganesh Vandana, a rhythmic piece with words and dance *bols* (syllables) in praise of the elephant-headed God. Gestures interpret the words that are interspersed with dance. This is followed by a brief dance prelude consisting of *Natwari bols* called *Amad* or the arrival/entry of the dancer, setting the mood and offering a formal salutation in the royal durbar.

Thaat, the first dance movement, begins with a graceful pose–the initial stance, with one foot crossed behind the other. The gaze is steady, the wrists are gently flexed sideways and body sways slightly. Delicate movements of brows, neck and wrists are in slow motion. The *ṭaal* gathers speed (usually the

16-beat Teentaal) and complex dance sequences called *tukras* or *toras* are rendered.

Chakkardar, the rapid turning movements accented by the feet is the usual climax of dance patterns that end precisely on the *sum*.

Kavita is a short poem interspersed with groups of rhythm syllables in the text. It is a dance composition interpreted with gestures and rhythm patterns.

Gat Bhava is the art of story-telling in expressive mime and dance. The dancer is not restricted to recited verse and rhythm syllables, but has freedom to depict the theme in rhythmic mime and dance within the framework of the *tala* played on the tabla.[6]

The climax of a Kathak dance recital is *Tatkaar*, a display of complex footwork in multiples of the *tala* of 16 beats–quadruple, octuple and the fastest possible speed called *anudruta*. Technical skill in fast footwork overlaid with cross rhythms is a mark of a dancer's proficiency.

Kathakali

The dance is a vital part of Kathakali dance-drama. Pure dance of classical quality precedes the performance of the play and dance sequences called *kalasams* provide the framework for dramatic expression (*abhinaya*). The *kalasam* is a dance finale or interlude at the end of a dramatic theme.

In Kathakali, the basic positions of the limbs and feet and their movements have technical conventions as exacting as the ballet of the West. The knees are bent in the characteristic stance and the feet set wide apart, toes pointing forward. The outer side of the sole rests on the ground. The manner of stepping in a wide stance, beating the heels and raising the feet is different from other forms of Indian classical dance. The wide stance and the dynamic flexion of the torso from side to side in the *atibhanga* flexion or great bend gives to Kathakali its basic qualities–strength and vitality. Formal dance gestures are the alternating allapadma or 'lotus' hand and *samdama* (thumb and first finger joined) and the *ardha-chandra* and *vardhamanaka* hands. These hand symbols have different names in Kathakali texts.[7]

Feminine Dance Mode of Kathakali

The feminine style of dance called Sari usually introduces a principal female character. It begins with a wide stance, arms raised and elbows bent. The torso sways from side to side with a sliding step, eyebrows fluttered, facial expression erotic. With a creeping movement of the feet the dancer moves forward and poses. In the exposition of a dramatic theme, there are brief interludes of dance–the wide stance and steps tracing a rectangular path in slow and double timing, ending in a *kalasam*.

The movement of the eyes is of great importance in Kathakali. They express the eight sentiments of Kathakali dance-drama and are according to the text of the *Natya Sastra*. Controlled movements of the eyeballs are acquired by a long disciplined practice of eye exercises. These movements are circular, diagonal, vertical (up and down), horizontal, fluttering, sidelong, projected and drawn in. The eyes move steadily and are completely independent of the eyelids which remain open.

Breath control is also of great significance. It is essential for the exposition of the more intense sentiments. In the erotic mood, the breath moves equally in and out to indicate passion. In sudden fury, the breath is suspended, the ribs are expanded and rigid. The diaphragm pulsates in sorrow and laughter.

Odissi

Odissi, the dance of ceremonial gestures and mimed song has existed for at least a thousand years in Orissa. It was the Maharis who brought this dance form into existence in the temples of Orissa and it was thus accorded a high spiritual status. Even to this day, the Maharis perform Odissi as part of the rituals of the Jagannath temple at Puri.

The *Abhinaya Chandrika*, an old palm-leaf manuscript of the 12th century AD, defines every element of Odissi dance in choreographic terms and compares in many ways to the *Natya Shastra* texts. The text details about 58 hand gestures and each of the *bhangis* (bends) of Odissi have specific names and detailed description.

As per tradition, the dance begins with obeisance to the deity–an erect pose with folded hands. This is followed by obeisance to the earth *(Bhumi Pranam)* in a semi-seated pose with *Sikhara* hands placed on the ground and when raised, touching the forehead. The completion of the ceremony is the flower offering or *Pushpanjali*. The *Ganesh Vandana* follows this. *Batu Nritya,* which is a dance dedicated to Siva, comes next. It combines pure dance and ritual offerings. The dance is characterized by intoned rhythm syllables, intricate movements of the feet and accentuated supple movements of the rest of the body. The accompaniment for this is drums and cymbals. A fast, swinging rhythm brings the dance to a climax.

The *Ishtadeva Vandana,* which follows, is a hymn or Sanskrit *shloka* in praise of the deity. Mimetic gestures convey the meaning and facial expression, the mood (*bhava*).

An interlude of pure dance, *Pallavi Nritta*, interprets patterns of melody and passages of rhythm syllables in beautifully syncronised movements and steps. Final sequences of the dance are in a fast, swinging, triple-rhythm, set in a four-beat timing. The dance ends in a rhythmic finale.

Any chosen song is then rendered with expository mime (*Gita Abhinaya*). The ritual closes with *Taarijhum*, a dance in fast tempo.[8]

The Odissi dance repertoire includes two dances in a joyous mood–*Nartana* and *Natangi*. Less formal in style, these dances delight in rounded curves and flexions of sculptural beauty. *Nartana* creates the joyous mood for the gesture song which follows and is accompanied by melody and dance syllables. In *Natangi,* intricately chanted rhythms in unison with the drum are gracefully rendered. The last part of the dance is called *Jhula* (swing) because of its swinging rhythm (three beats) and the swaying of hips.

Music in Odissi Dance

Odissi incorporates the form of "visualized music" of the *ragas* and *raginis* of Classical Indian music. At several points in the history of this dance form, efforts were made to classify Odissi music as a style distinct from both Hindustani and Carnatic. Such efforts have not borne fruit as yet, but perhaps like Odissi the dance form, the music too will some day earn the status of another form of classical music.

The noted musician-dramatist of the 15th century, Ramananda Patnaik, popularly referred to as Rai Ramananda, is said to have had a major hand in the blossoming of this form of music. In Odissi, the danseuse first describes the *raga* in gestures interpreting a poem (*raga swaroop*). Since musical theory ascribes each *raga* melody to a specific mood, season, time of the day and each note of the scale is identified with the cry of a bird or animal, the dancer attempts to describe them. The scale form is then sung, with each note symbolizing the cry of a bird or animal shown through hand gestures.

A *swara pallavi* dance usually forms a prelude to the gesture-song interpreting the poem of that particular *raga.* Usually, different couplets of the song are set in different *talas,* with some of the common ones being *Ektaal* (four beats), *Triputa* (seven beats) and *Khemta* (three beats).

Among the numerous melodies sung in Odissi, the all-time favourites include the erotic theme songs of Radha and Krishna from the *Geet Govinda* of Jayadev and the *Champu* songs of Kavisurya Baladeva Rath.

Kuchipudi

Kuchipudi has grown from strength to strength in a little over 50 years. From a little-known local tradition practiced by Brahmins in an Andhra Pradesh village, this dance form has acquired a large audience and its character has also undergone several changes over the years. Modern-day Kuchipudi now has a majority of female exponents as against the traditional male dominance.

Though there is architectural evidence that dance existed

as a regular part of entertainment way back in the 2nd century B.C., historical evidence of this form dates back to roughly the 16th century B.C. According to Leela Venkatraman and Avinash Pasricha in their book *Indian Classical Dance: Tradition in transition*, "While the learning and Sanskrit knowledge required by the Kuchipudi actor are cited as having dictated the Brahmin emphasis, it is clear the art form acquired its character because of the nature of the performers who came from a Sanskrit background. The Kuchipudi *Bhagavatulu* (dancers) specialised not only in dance drama of *Yakshagana*, but also in a special category of opera called *Kalapams*. *Kalapams* were a form of total theatre interwoven with a structure of musical compositions called Daru-s, all relating to one theme. *Bhama Kalapam*, portraying the mercurial Satyabhama, a consort of Krishna, in her diverse moods is Kuchipudi's piece de resistance. Siddhendra Yogi and Narayan Tirtha are considered the two great preceptors of Kuchipudi and are known for having composed the bulk of most widely-acclaimed Kuchipudi dance pieces.

Curiously, in what was an all-male tradition, female roles like those of Satyabhama, Rukmini, Mohini etc. were pre-eminent. *Streevesham*, with its cross-gender impersonation carried much weight.

The role of the actor in Kuchipudi included spoken bits of dialogue and even sung passages. This comprehensive singing, acting and dancing prowess of the performer has now been changed to a largely dance-oriented expertise. The vocalist in the team of musicians accompanying the performance has taken over all the singing. As for the dialogue passages in Telugu, they have become rare among urban dancers coming from a variety of backgrounds. Only in the traditional *Yakshagana* presentation by the village troupes does one get to hear the spoken passages. The only exception in the contemporary scene of a dancer who can sing, speak and dance the *Kalapams* is Swapnasundari. She has probed the Andhra *devadasi* solo tradition and worked at reconstructing the dance, now called *Vilasini Natyam*."

In Kuchipudi, the movement does not have one central stance round which the technique revolves. The half-seated position, with the knees flexed sideways, is much used, but not as the main stylistic concern as in Bharatanatyam. But movements are repeated on both sides of the body as in Bharatanatyam. There is a springy graceful up and down movement, with the dancer constantly changing levels with frequent weight shifts – the foot-contact continually changing with flat feet touching the floor or heels, toes and even the side of the feet tapping the floor. Moving forward with the big toe of the two feet interlocked is a typical gait, as is executing rhythm patterns in the crossed feet position. This is a vigorous dance form and doesn't have place for the slow movements that other dance forms incorporate.

The dance-music relationship is also less structured than in other dances and often a one-line repetitive musical backdrop which provides a lilt and emphasizes a mood, sees the dancer presenting an entire narrative sequence or canvas of mime and rhythm woven into the tala cycle. The walk in Kuchipudi has a characteristic saucy and sensuous grace. A characteristic of this dance form is that of the dancer holding the tip of her decorated braid in her left hand. In fact, the dancer's braid plays a significant role in stating her supremacy.

Today, the man enacting a woman's role has become rare. The sophisticated urban version of the dance form now owes much to Vempati Chinna Satyam under whom a long line of now-established dancers have been trained. He is also credited for having introduced other ragas as part of the music repertoire for Kuchipudi, apart from the usual list of favourites like Mohanam, Mukhari, Bhairavi and Todi.

It is significant to note that till the 1958 Sangeet Natak Akademi Festival, there was not slot for this dance form except for a short demonstration by a dancer named Kanchanamala. It is only in 1959, after the Andhra Pradesh Sangeet Natak Akademi organised a seminar on supporting the case for making Kuchipudi a classical dance form that it got taken seriously. Indrani Rehman and Yamini Krishnamurthy popularized the dance form globally and dancersfrom non-traditional backgrounds like Raja and Radha Reddy began to set up flourishing Kuchipudi schools.

THEATRE

Folk Performances–The Basis of Indian Theatre

It is generally perceived that theatre in India has its origin in her villages. Many believe it is an art that is total–having within its realm music, dance, movement, dialogue and, of course, acting. The audience of a folk play usually participates in the play. In fact, both the actor and the audience are co-participants in what is ultimately a shared religious ritual in the form of a play. Some believe that folk theatre is the expression through song, dance, chants, words and music of the needs and requirements of the tribal or village community, for the community. Quite often, all the members of the rustic community take part in the performing process. Performances are usually for the gods or for nature or for the community itself and sometimes for all three. Folk performances grow out of rites and rituals going back to antiquity. They are part of the lifestyle of the village or tribal community, intimately linked to agricultural cycle of the life of the peasants, whether it is sowing, reaping or harvesting. Besides, certain "classes" among the villagers are specially skilled in the presentation of folk performances, whether it is the Vairagis, the Binkaras, the Bhavaiyas, the Bauls, etc. These performers come from both "backward" and "elite" classes. In many, if not most village communities, there is hardly any distinction made between the participator, the actor-dancer, the musicians and the audience–all join in. These performances are not for sale or commercial use–they have a ritualistic and communitarian function. They could be performances that help the community to be free of disease, come to terms with death, to commemorate ancestors, to invoke a good harvest, etc.

Folk vs Urban Theatre

During the '50s and '60s, an awareness began to grow among our young urban theatre workers of the complex and rich forms of Indian folk theatre. Under the stewardship of Dr. Suresh Awasthi, the Sangeet Natak Akademi (SNA) became the discoverer of a whole new area of folk-theatre traditions. Nautanki, Ramlila, Jatra, Bhavai were on every theatre exponent's lips and soon became household words to urban theatre workers. The Akademi decided to pitch in with grants for every, and any theatre elements or forms in their urban productions. It was a move to save the fast-dying folk traditions.

But in their attempt to make folk go urban, some glaring mistakes surfaced. May be the following aspects will help in getting a macro-view of the situation:

1. Folk performances take place in open, demarcated and "sacred" spaces. Urban theatre is mainly of the proscenium type, in a rented, enclosed hall, sometimes air-conditioned. The folk artiste literally treads on grass roots and is in touch with nature.

2. The audience participates in folk performances that take on ritualistic and sacred dimensions. They are cleansed, purified, recharged. The urban audience is a consumer audience which watches a two-hour entertainment for a price.

3. Folk performances take days, weeks or even months in terms of running time. They are performed on special days, "holy" days and equinoxes, full-moon nights and *sankrantis*. Urban theatre is just a two-hour show on stage and usually available on evenings.

4. Folk performances are not just presentations of skill, dance, music or song. They are a part of the life function of the community. They are ideological and in a way essential. Urban theatre (much of which is in English today) is entertainment or presentation of expertise unconnected with our life functions.

The Economics of Theatre

Doing theatre, compared to the art of writing, painting,

sculpting, singing or even filmmaking considering its market potential, is, far more expensive. Most significantly, theatre refuses to be duplicated. And, a stage performance every night involves a great amount of expenditure. Most of the time when a theatergoer buys a ticket, it actually just about covers the cost of the seat and the advertisements to notify him about the production. Add to that the cost of production–makeup, lighting, music, transport, refreshment, plus, the creative effort of 30 to 40 persons for months.

Tracing the economic cost of this creative pursuit, Rudraprasad Sengupta says in his article *The Economics of Good Theatre,* "The developed countries, both socialist and capitalist, by and large decided in favour of a comprehensive art patronage system at the time of the Second World War. In most of these countries, the state subsidized 60 per cent of the costs and the remaining 40 per cent was taken care of by the box office. In fact, the socialist countries attached greater importance to theatre. Contrast this with the Indian scenario where the Sangeet Natak Akademi offers meager sums of money to various performing arts organizations."

Recently, the corporate sector has come forward with some funds. The Tatas have established the massive National Centre for the Performing Arts in Mumbai and the Sri Ram Centre is another such endeavour in New Delhi. But most of the time artistes are expected to settle for crumbs, while funds mainly go into advertising.[9]

A lot of theatre groups in India, therefore, apply to foreign foundations working here for financial assistance. Their help is frequently not only more substantial, but also less caught up in the red tape and obligations that go hand in hand with our domestic agencies, whether private or public.

Music in Theatre: The entire edifice of Marathi theatre today stands on the foundation of "music theatre"–Sangit Natak. Pioneers like Vishnu Das Bhave, lived in an area where Kannada was spoken and both had access to Kannada theatre. Perhaps it was Yakshagana that inspired them in some way and Yakshagana is full of music. Going back further, we will find that Yakshagana practitioners, specially those from south Karnataka, drew their inspiration from something like Krishnattam, Kutiyattam or Kathakali which had existed earlier. There too, music plays a very crucial role. This means that most of what we know as Indian theatre is based on the idea of music as an integral part of theatre. Yet in recent times one finds a Western categorization. There is what one calls "legitimate" theatre, thereby classifying theatre with music as "illegitimate" perhaps. The "legitimate" may also be called the bookish, wordy theatre. Most of the theatre in urban centers is legitimate. Partisans of this kind of theatre look down upon the use of music.

In Maharashtra, in the third and fourth decades of this century, there grew a feeling that it was music that was becoming a millstone around the neck of good theatre. "Legitimate" theatre was suffocating, gasping. Nothing worthwhile was being written, nothing worthwhile was being staged because of the earlier legacy of such great singer-actors like Bal Gandharva and Dinanath Kolhatkar. A backlash developed and a definite movement was launched to see music out of the way. Certainly many issues were addressed through the new theatre; they had more realistic plots because it was now possible to have theatre without music. But no one in those days seems to have wondered that just as plays, themes and issues changed, so could music in plays also change from one kind to another.

Music adds to the atmosphere in theatre. In his essay, *The Meaningful and Dramatic in Theatre Music*, well-known theatreperson, Bhaskar Chandravarkar says: "It acts on one level like a conveyor of specific emotions. Take the world-renowned opera *Carmen*, composed by Bizet. It has been staged in different languages and sometimes the occupations of the characters in the opera have also been changed. But the music remained. By itself, the story is nothing much to write home about. But because of the music composition, the play has become a classic over generations."[10]

In other plays too, it is the music that gives people a new

level of experience, a new dimension to the story. And each time people see and hear the same play, they listen to something they have not been able to hear earlier.

REFERENCES

1. *The Tradition of the Performing Arts*; Dr. Kapila Vatsyayan, National Centre for the Performing Arts, Quarterly Journal, March 1975.
2. *Invitation to Indian Music*; Shakuntala Narasimhan, Arnold-Heinemann Publishers.
3. *Dance Dialectics of India*; Ragini Devi, Motilal Banarasidas Publishers.
4. *Ibid.*
5. *Ibid.*
6. *Ibid.*
7. *Ibid.*
8. *Ibid.*
9. *The Economics of 'Good' Theatre;* Rudraprasad Sengupta, *Rasa–The Indian Performing Arts in the Last 25 Years,* Anamika Kala Sangam Research and Publications, Kolkata.
10. *The Meaningful and Dramatic in Theatre Music;* Bhaskar Chandravarkar, *Rasa–The Indian Performing Arts in the Last 25 Years,* Anamika Kala Sangam Research and Publications, Kolkata.

2

Aesthetics in Hindustani Music

Raag, Forms of Hindustani Music and a Good Performance

Indian music is essentially melodic. Folk, Vedic chants and pure classical music–all these forms have the common quality of being based on melody. Ages of experimentation and artistic development of the melody have given us the concept of '*raag*', which is the fundamental basis of Indian musical tradition and, therefore, of Hindustani classical music.

A '*raag*' may be defined broadly as a melodic scheme, characterized by a definite scale of notes (alphabet) set in a sequence, melodic phrases, pauses and tonal graces. Emotional appeal is, of course, a prime requisite.

A melody is a flow of sound–up and down, with various rhythmic distributions. When we abstract these characteristics and make a 'type', it becomes a *raag*–a musical language. Here again, out of a stream of sound, 'notes' are created and named, and a particular arrangement of these 'notes' becomes a '*raag*'. The visual representation of such musical symbols is the notation.

In music, we have set musical sounds called notes or *swaras*. One *swara* is different from another by being 'higher' or 'lower'. That is, *swaras* differ from one another in pitch. In all, there are 12 notes in the generalized musical alphabet, arranged as under:

Sa, Re, Ga, Ma, Pa, Dha, Ni = *shuddha swaras*

ri ga ma dha ni = *vikrita swaras*

In delineating a *'raag'*, a musician will ordinarily not use a *swara* not proper to it. Such notes are called *varjya swaras*. Every *raag* therefore, has its own alphabet of notes, which it neither exceeds nor reduces. Based on this principle, *raag*s are divided into various *jatis* (types), depending on the number of notes they have. The simplest types are the *oudava* (five notes–pentatonic), *shadava* (six notes, hexatonic) and *sampoorna* (seven notes, heptatonic). Besides the notes and their order, there are certain characteristic phrases always occurring in a *'raag'* which give it its melodic form. They have to be repeated and emphasized so that the uniqueness of the *'raag'* is made clear. Such phrases are called *pakad, anga, varna,* etc.

Certain *swaras* find emphasis in varying degrees (*vadi, samvadi, anuvadi*). Melodic sections commence and end on defined notes (*graha* and *nyasa*).

While there are graces and accents common to all *raag*s, most of them have *gamakas* all their own, which give them distinct qualities.

There are species and varieties of *raag*s. But each can expand only into its own form. However, no particular rendering of it is identical to any other. Two renderings of the same *raag* are essentially similar, but different in detail owing to the temperament of the musician and the mood of the situation.

The time theory in Hindustani classical music is of great significance and applicable to this day. Though there is a debate on the time of rendition of certain ancient and modern *raag*s, in a majority of cases the time theory still prevails. Broadly classified, the time theory slots *raag*s as 1. *Sandhiprakash raags* are *komal re* and *komal* dha *raag*s 2. *Shuddha re* and *shuddha dha raags* and 3. *Komal ga* and *komal ni raags*.

Sandhiprakash Raags

*Raag*s which use *komal re* and *komal dha* in their scale are known as *sandhiprakash raags*. One of the prerequisites of this scale is that along with the *komal re* and *komal dha*, it is necessary to have *tivra ga*. *Komal ga* with this combination of two notes will transfer the *raag* to the third category. The time when it is neither day nor night is known as *sandhi-kaal*. *Raag*s that are rendered at this time are known as *sandhiprakash raags* like Bhairav, Kalingada, Bhairavi, Poorvi, Marwa, etc. These are further divided into *pratahkalin sandhiprakash raags* and *sainkalin sandhiprakash raag*s, referring to those that are sung in the morning and evening respectively.

Madhyam is the most important note in these *raag*s. The rule is that the *pratahkalin sandhiprakash raag*s have *shuddha madhyam*, while the *sainkalin sandhiprakash raag*s have *teevra madhyam*. For example, Bhairav and Kalingada are morning *raag*s using *shuddha madhyam* and Poorvi and Marwa, which are evening *raag*s, employ *teevra madhyam*.

The other characteristic of such *raag*s is that *dhaivat* may be *komal* or *teevra*, but *komal rishabh* and *teevra gandhar-nishad* are a must. But critics are normally aware that Bhairavi is an exception.

Shuddha Re-Dha Raags

Such *raag*s are normally rendered after those which are *sandhiprakash*. Like the above group of *raag*s, this too features twice within the 24-hour cycle. *Raag*s of the Kalyan and Bilawal that fall within this category. The time slot for these *shuddha rishabh-dhaivat raag*s ranges from seven to 10 in the day and night alternatively. *Shuddha gandhar* and *madhyam* are important notes in such scales. *Raag*s such as Yaman, Shuddha Kalyan, Deshkar and Bilawal are examples of this category.

Komal Ga-ni Raags

This is the third variety of *raag*s which are rendered after the time for the *shuddha Re-Dha raag*s get over. Their main characteristic is that *Ga* has necessarily to be *komal*, irrespective of whether *Re* and *Dha* are *shuddha* or *komal*. Their rendition timing is between 10 in the morning to four in the afternoon and the next block is from 10 at night to four in the morning. Yaman, Baageshri, Jaijaiwanti and Malkauns are some of the *raags* that feature in this category. Due to the paucity of morning concerts, one unfortunately does not get to hear a lot of the *raags* as it is still fairly common for both musicians and listeners to adhere to the above-mentioned time theory. As most concerts are scheduled in the evening, the number of, say, Yaman renditions would far outnumber Todi presentations. Hopefully, organizers and listeners will both make it convenient for morning and afternoon concerts to flourish. The only other source of hearing such *raags* becomes All India Radio or some pre-recorded cassettes. Most television channels also choose to relegate their classical music programmes to late nights, where again, only a handful of *raags* can be heard.

Important notes in a *raag*:

ग्रहांशौ तारमंद्रो च षाडचौडाबेते तथा।

अल्पत्वं च बहुतवं च न्यासो पन्यास एव च

Matanga's *Brihaddeshi* has classified the important notes of a *raag* as 10. They are:[1]

1. *Graha:* It is the note that is used in the beginning of the song. It is an alternative term for Amsa.

2. *Amsa:* It is the prominent note in the song. The peculiar charm, that is the melodic version of the song depends on it. It is the basis for the limit of the employment of notes in the high and the low registers. It is perceived prominently (in many combinations of notes) and is used as the Graha, Apanyasa, Vinyasa, Samanyasa and Nyasa.

   Matanga points out the difference between Graha and Amsa. The former may be the sonant, consonant, assonant or dissonant, but the latter is always the sonant. The difference is understood also as *Amsa* being the principal and *Graha*, the subordinate.

3. *Tara*: The limit of the notes to be used in the high register is the fourth note from Amsa or the 5th note. According to the reading given by Matanga, it may be the seventh note also.

4. *Mandra*: The limit of the notes to be used in the lower register is the Amsa or the Nyasa or the Apanyasa note.
5. *Nyasa:* It is the note with which the song ends.
6. *Apanyasa*: It is the note on which the division of the song ends. The terms Samanyasa and Vinyasa occur in the definition of Amsa.
7. *Alpatva*: It is the use of a note or notes in small measure. It is two-fold–by skipping over the particular note or notes, e.g. in hexatonic and pentatonic treatment and by non-repitition. The non-repitition is to be made of the notes which are not the Amsa notes. Skipping over a note may also be carried out by not employing the note fully.
8. *Bahutva*: It is of two kinds–by using the note fully or by repeating it often.
9. *Sadavitva*: Six notes are used, omitting one note. The consonant note of that note which is dropped is employed.
10. *Audavitva*: Five notes are employed, dropping two notes having consonance.

In later years, when the *raag* system of categorization of melodies replaced the *Jati* system, most of these notes remained in a diluted form. The *Raag* system employed terms like *Vaadi, Samvaadi, Anuvadi, Varjya* etc.

वादी स्वरास्तु राजा स्यानमन्त्री संवादीसंगीत

स्वरो विवादी बैरी स्यादनुवादी च श्रुतयावात

What this means is that the *Vaadi swara* is considered the King, *samvaadi* the Minister, *Vivaadi* the enemy and *Anuvaadi* the *sewak* or servant.

Raag and *Jati*

Currently, *raag*s are popularly classified into *Jatis*. In fact, one of the prime characteristics of a *raag* is its *Jati*. It has been classified on the basis of the number of notes used in the ascendant and descendent scales.

1. When a *raag* uses all seven notes, irrespective of whether they are *shuddha, komal* or *teevra*, it is classified as having *Sampoorna Jati.*

2. When a *raag* uses six notes, it has a *Saadav Jati.*

3. A *raag* using five notes in the scale, both in ascending and descending order is known to have an *Audav Jati.*

4. The three above mentioned categories refer to *raags* having the same number of notes both in ascending and descending order. The next set of *Jatis* takes into account *raags* which may have all seven notes in the ascending and six in the descent. Such *raags* are said to have *Sampoorna-Saadav Jatis.*

5. Similarly, there are *raags* that have six notes in the ascent and five in the descent. Such *raags* take on the *Saadav-Audav Jati.*

Therefore, depending on how a *raag*'s scale is formed, its *Jati* is defined looking at the number of notes employed.

The *Rasa* Theory of Hindustani Classical Music

The ancient, medieval and modern texts have at least a chapter devoted to the *rasa* theory of Hindustani music. However, the reality is that most musicians find it hard to keep pace with the practical aspect of this subject and do not have the time to be well versed with the theory of music. The usefulness of this theory, however, cannot be emphasized enough. Without its practical application, all music would sound extremely mechanical.

Music is a form of art which brings unbridled joy to both the listener and performer even in the midst of unhappiness. The only way that this can be accentuated is by the use of expression of emotion.

As it stimulates the emotions, it becomes imperative for *raags* to have *rasa*. Therefore, it stands to reason that *raag* and *rasa* go hand in hand. There are nine *rasas* in music which have been described below. It becomes important to throw light on them when analyzing classical music from a critic's point of view. A critic would normally listen to a recital keeping this *rasa* theory in mind to gauge the depth of the artiste's feelings and involvement with a particular *raag*.

Shaant rasa: When man wants some reprieve from the sadness, pressures and tensions of daily life, he seeks peace of mind. This act of seeking peace of mind through music is *shaant rasa*. A *raag* which spurs you on towards this feeling of detachment and, in the process, towards peace of mind, is *shaant*

Karun rasa: This *rasa* embodies a feeling of sadness where an individual moves from a state of gain to loss. The underlying emotion is sadness–whether it is the loss of a loved one or grief over any issue.

Bhakti rasa: The praise, devotion and awe for the almighty, his several incarnations, their deeds and their glorification fall within this category of *bhakti rasa*.

Vaatsalya rasa: This ascribes to the love a parent has for his/her child. The offspring's *atics,* achievements, idiosyncrasies and mischief become topics to be recounted.

Veer rasa: This *rasa* is a reflection of courage and valour. Through its elaboration and musical portrayal, optimism is generated and a fighting spirit is inculcated.

Haasya, Adbhut, Raudra, Vibhatsa and ***Bhayanak rasas***: It is difficult for an artiste, whether vocalist or instrumentalist to exclusively express any of these emotions. It is also difficult to pinpoint a *raag* which is an expression of specifically one of these rasas.

Haasya rasa is depiction of humour, mischief and laughter. It lends itself to a certain flightiness and friskiness in the music.

Adbhut, or anything which astonishes, results from amazement caused by something unusual happening.

Raudra or anger is the *rasa* which depicts rage in a person. What *raag* does, whether it is to just vent venom or go on a destructive spree, is at times brought to the forefront with the aid of music. However, as mentioned earlier, *raudra rasa* is also difficult to maintain in any particular *raag*.

Vibhatsa rasa denotes something that is disgusting. It often refers to something distorted, abnormal, ugly or dirty. It also brings forth the animality and crudeness of a situation to the fore.

Bhayanak or that which frightens, is yet another one of those *rasas* which become difficult to emote musically, especially in *raag* rendition. Musicologists thought of all possible human emotions and categorized them under nine heads.

Today, their application can be done in not just classical music, but also and probably more effectively, in commercial music. It is up to the artiste as to how this is executed and expressed through notes.

It is rather difficult to express *rasas* through individual notes, yet, according to Bharata, certain notes are used to express specific *rasas*.

मध्यमपंचम भूयिष्टं हास्यशृंगारयो भवेत्।
बङजर्षभ प्रायकृतं वीररौद्रद्भुतेषुच।।

He says *haasya* and *shringaar rasas* are produced by using *madhyam* and *pancham* frequently; *vira, adbhut* and *raudra rasas* are expressed through frequent use of *shadaja* and rishabh. This might be applicable to dramaturgy and background music provided by playing of instruments.

The *rasas* depend on various factors like tempo, tune and most importantly, the text of the song. As the text is an important factor related to the production of *rasa,* the clarity, tonal quality of voice and pronunciation are the indispensable components or assets of a musician.

Forms of Hindustani Classical Music

Dhruvapada

One of the most ancient forms of classical music is Dhruvapada, which many musicologists believe originated in the 15th century. According to most writers of the medieval period, Raja Mansingh of Gwalior (1468-1518) is said to be the person who originated this form. However, there isn't any definite proof of this. Another point of view is that a sophisticated and complex style of music such as *Dhruvapada* could not have been the invention of a single person. It most probably was the amalgamation of the talents of many musicians over a period of time. But the majority is of the opinion that Mansingh extended his full support and patronage to this style.

Tracing some of the forms of music from the 16th and 17th centuries in her book *Hindustani Music*, Dr. Najma Parveen Ahmad says: "An exhaustive study of our ancient texts proves that Dhruvpad evolved from the earlier forms of music which existed in our ancient musical system. Pt. Ratanjankar is of the opinion that Dhruvapad seems to be related to the tradition of religious hymns which were sung in the ancient temples. In some of the famous Vaishnavite temples of Dwarika and Jagannath Puri, singing and dancing before the deity was part of the daily ritual. Even today, the tradition is still alive. The songs, called *kirtans,* were sung in praise of God and were accompanied by the Mridang. The Sanskrit Prabandhas given in our ancient classical writings are more or less similar to these Kirtans. The *Gita Govinda* of Jaidev is also a collection of such *Prabandhas.* Then around the ninth century, Desi and Prakrit languages such as Brij Bhasha, Purvi, Bengali etc. started replacing Sanskrit. As part of this change, famous poets of the Bhakti period such as Chaitanya Mahaprabhu, Vidyapati, Baiju Bawra, Swami Haridas, etc. composed songs in these languages which were sung in the temples. These songs were well-composed and provided scope for *aalaap* and *layakari.* Based on the structure of these songs, the court singers developed songs in the new Dhruvapada styles that had an emphasis on the aesthetic aspects.

A close examination of the characteristics of *Prabandha* described in *Sangeet Ratnakar* are comparable to the characteristics of Dhruvapad.

The word *Dhruvapada* is a combination of two words–*Dhruva* and *Pada.* Anything that is fixed or immovable refers to *Dhruva. Pada* means the verbal text. *Dhruvapada* can be divided into different *dhatus* or four parts–*sthaayi, antara, sanchari* and *aabhog.* In some of these compositions, one or two parts are missing. It is normally sung in Chautaal, Sulphak, Jhampa, Teevra or Rudrataal. It is characterized by the absence of *taan,* but it features *dugun, chaugun* of rhythm and the use of *boltaan.*

According to the *Anoop Sangeet Ratnakar* written by Bhavbhatta, *Dhruvapada* is a *Pad* which is composed in the language endemic to Madhya Pradesh. It has two or four *Tuks* (metres), narrating the theme of love dominated by *Shringar Ras,* the essence of which is infused with *aalaap.* According to Bhavbhatta, the different parts of *Dhruvapada* have been given the same name as in *Prabandha.* The importance and glory of this form is also manifest under Mughal rulers Akbar, Aurangzeb and Jahangir, through compositions rendered by some of their famous court musicians.

A systematic study of *Dhruvapada* reveals that this form of singing has evolved during the last eight centuries and has gone through several refinements. Even today, it is a popular form of classical music and still retains its artistic structure.

Khayal

This is the most popular form of classical music. It is characterized by an introductory *aalaap,* followed by a *vilambit khayal.* This is then carried on further by *aalaap* rendition, while singing the *bandish* and concluding it with the *mukhda* and showing the *sum.* A short *boltaan* session follows and it is rounded off with tans using different patterns. This form in the *vilambit khayal* is repeated in the *drut khayal,* which finally concludes the *raag* rendition.

A detailed discussion on *Khayal* will follow in the forthcoming chapters.

Tarana

Today, *Tarana* refers to a form of singing in which certain selected syllables devoid of meaning are repetitively interwoven and recited in any *raag*. The modern version of the *Tarana* does not have any individual identity of its own and is generally treated as a part of the *Khayal* style. But an analysis of its historical past reveals that it was a distinct and advanced style of music having its own important place in the musical system as indicated in the important works written during the medieval period.

Amir Khusrau is generally credited as the originator of *Tarana*. According to Dr. Najma Ahmad in her book *Hindustani Music*, "*Tohfat-ul-Hind*, written in the eighteenth century, describes *Tarana* as having Arabic and Persian couplets in which few meaningless syllables are repeated in various melodious forms. The principles and structure of this style have been derived from Hindustani *Geet*. The *Tarana* has been equated with the *Tillana* in this book. However, *Tillana* is primarily associated with Karnataka style of music. It is sung both as a composition and is also sung as accompaniment to dance. But *Tarana* has been associated with the *Khayal* style of Hindustani music and is considered an integral part of vocal music. Today, *Tarana* is just an ornamental part of *Khayal* singing. But earlier, *Tarana* included Persian and Arabic couplets which were decorated with syllables like *Ta, Re, Da, Ni* etc.

There could be a debate as to whether Amir Khusrau was solely the inventor of the *Tarana* or whether it existed in Arabic and Persian systems of music as a composition. At this juncture it is worth pointing out that in Arabic music, there was mention of a form of music called *Nauba*, even before the 10th century A.D. *Nauba* was based on four parts, and one of these was *Tarana*. So, it would be appropriate to say that Amir Khusrau probably introduced this style of singing into Hindustani music and it was based on existing patterns found in Hindustani music as well as other musical systems. In his *Tarana* compositions, Khusrau has introduced the *Qaul* form of singing as well."[2]

Although this style was introduced sometime in the 14th century, it did not acquire as much recognition in the royal courts. However, it was popular in musical sittings of Sufis and religious gatherings at tombs of saints. It found more listeners in the latter half of the 17th and 18th centuries, like the *Khayal*. Several *Tarana* compositions are to be found in *Nadirat-e-Ṣhahi*, which was written during the above-mentioned period, under the reign of Shah Alam.

Three types of *Taranas* were in vogue then (and much of that pattern still persists today). They are:

Compositions having the syllables of *Tarana* in the *Sthayi* and *Antara*.

Compositions having the *Tarana* syllables in the *Sthayi* and Persian and Urdu couplets in the *Antara*.

Compositions having *Tarana* syllables in the *Sthayi* and syllables of *Trivat* in the *Antara*.

Other Forms

Then there are the so-called semi-classical forms like *Qawwali, Thumri, Daadra,* which are somewhat diluted in terms of *raag* purity. *Qawwali* is often in praise of the almighty and mostly has a singer and chorus team. *Thumri*s epitomize the element of shringaar in music. Each of these forms have well-defined presentation patterns which vary from one region of India to the other.

Music as Performing Art

Art, whether painting, sculpture, dance or theatre, is largely visual. The prime stimulant of the mind in all these forms is the eye. Music on the other hand, is essentially dependant on the ear. The purity of the notes is perceived through the sense of hearing. However, it is only when this form of art is performed live in front of an audience that the true impact of its artistry becomes evident.

The fact that music is a performing art has been established since almost the beginning of time. People used to gather in groups and sing or play an instrument for pure listening pleasure and amusement. Those who were more tuneful than the others were asked to present the same piece again and again or to perform something new.

With the advent of kings and kingdoms, most of these musicians received royal patronage. Some took to performing music as a whole-time job. Others would sing/play as a hobby. Most of the time the king would take on the responsibility of looking after not just the musician, but also his entire family. And as time went by, music became more and more refined with due recognition by the State. The number of listeners grew and so did the compositions and *raag*s.

At present, music enjoys the patronage of the government and some business houses. However, the audience is largely an invited one. There are very few concerts which are ticketed. Most of the time it is a handful of artistes who circulate as performers, and ironically, they and they alone are the ones who draw the maximum crowds.

The stage, therefore, has become the most prestigious place for a performance. True, cassettes, CDs and videos are other means of broadcasting music, but a live performance in front of an audience is what makes music. What the artiste wears, his/her stage presence and mannerisms, all contribute in making a good performance. Sometimes what the artiste says in the midst of a recital can also provide insight and entertainment. Of course, what the artiste performs is the essence. But many times a performance venue and the audience itself can be inspirational forces for the artiste's performance. Because of this mutually beneficial status, music thrives as a performing art.

Since we are studying the various aspects of music criticism, we should know what is the ideal in musicianship. This will be the basis for deciding what is good music and what is bad. There are several musicologists who have enlisted what in their view is a good singer and what constitutes bad music. Each of them has devoted at least a chapter to this.

Some of these music texts on music have listed out a few characteristics of what a good performer ought to have. Let us look at what two such manuscripts have to say.

In terms of vocal music, the parameters are clearly listed out as follows by Sharangdev in his book *Sangeet Ratnakar*:

हृधशब्दुः सुशारीरो ग्रहमोक्षविचक्षणः ।
रागरागांगभाषांगक्रियांगोपांगकोबिदः ।।
प्रबंधगाननिष्णातो बिबिधालप्तितच्ववित् ।
सर्वस्थानोच्चगमकेवनायासलसद्गतिः ।।
आयत्तकंठस्तालज्ञः सावधानो जितश्रयः ।
शुद्धच्छायालगाभिज्ञः सर्वकाकुविशेषवित् ।।
अपारस्थायसंचारः सर्वदोपविषर्जितः ।
क्रियापरोऽजस्रलयः सुघटो धारणान्वितः ।।
स्फूर्जन्निर्जवनो हारिरहः कृद्रमजनोद्धुरः ।
सुसम्पदायो गीतज्ञैर्गीयते गायनाग्रणीः ।।

Some of the characteristics as mentioned in the *shloka* are:

1. Someone who has a sweet and melodious voice.
2. A person whose vocal chords can reproduce a particular '*raag*'s' scale without prior practice.
3. The person who knows the usage of the *graha* (the note on which the *raag* commences), *nyaas* (the note on which the *raag* concludes) and *anksha* (the note which is predominantly used in *raag* expansion) *swaras*.
4. The individual should be knowledgeable about the raag-raginis (the ancient classification of *raags*).
5. He can please the listeners with his music.
6. He has received guidance from a guru of high caliber.
7. He should be imaginative.
8. He should have perfect rhythm sense.
9. The musician must be doing regular *riyaaz*.
10. He should be one who has great concentration and does not waver from the *raag* expansion.

Likewise, some of the characteristics of a poor performer according to the *Sangeet Ratnakar* are as follows:

1. He/she sings with teeth clenched.
2. Doesn't have soul in his music and sings with a harsh voice.
3. Lacks confidence while singing.
4. His/her voice shakes while singing.
5. Makes faces while singing.
6. Has a voice as harsh as a crow's.
7. The singer uses notes that are not accurate–a shruti up or down.
8. One who gesticulates wildly while singing.
9. A singer who confuses and mixes *raag*s in his performance.
10. And one whose singing has a nasal sound.

The ancient texts define what a perfect musician is. The term *uttam vagyakaar* is used to describe one. It is the merger of two terms *vaak* and *gey. Vaak* means the skill in writing/ pronouncing lyrics, while *gey* denotes music composition.

In other words, a person who is a good singer/ instrumentalist and is knowledgeable about the lyrics/words being used, is considered the ultimate *vagyekaar*. In the western music world, such talented persons were given the title of composers.

In *Sangeet Makaranda,* the characteristics of V*aggeyakara* begin without any *prelude* or introduction, under *Gayaka lakshanam.* Only the concluding *shloka* says that these are the qualities of a *Vaggeyakara.* The 28 qualities listed here are similar to those mentioned in the *Sangeet Ratnakara.*

The merits of a musician and good singing are defined by almost all the authors, ancient and modern. In *Sangeet Ratnakara* it has taken a much more developed form. Narada of *Naradiya*

Shiksha describes the properties and merits of good music in these words:

गानस्यत्तु दशविधा गुणवृत्तिस्तदस्तद् यथा

रक्तं पूर्णमलंकृतं प्रसन्नं व्यक्तं विक्रुष्टम्

श्लक्षणं समं सुकुमारं मधुरमिति गुणा:।

He describes the 10 qualities, which are:

Raktam: It means tunefulness. The ability to produce a similar voice to the Veena and Venu. The voice should merge with the flute and the *Veena. Purnam*–The word means perfection or fullness. The music should be perfectly in co-ordination with metre, note and tune. On the lyrical side, the words should be well pronounced and the division of syllables should be well-adjusted to the music.

Prasannam: It means the voice of the singer should be clear and effortless and without any strain.

Vyaktam: The meaning of the song should be clear and the pronunciation of the words should be expressive. The syllables of the words should be pronounced and divided carefully.

Vikrushtam: To pronounce the words, their syllables and letters clearly in the upper register or high pitch.

Shlakshanam: The word means smooth, delicate or polished. When the musician blends the different *layas,* upper and lower notes, long and short syllables with a smooth tone, it is called *shlakshanam.*

Samam: It means equal. The starting and ending notes of the songs are always fixed. When these are handled according to the rules, it is called *samam.*

Sukumaram: This indicates the delicate and musical application of voice and pronunciation of the words effortlessly, without harshness.

Madhuram: It means sweetness. Natural sweetness of the song pronounced by a happy and sweet voice.

The Making of a Good Performance

The concept of a good performance changes with time. It also changes, depending on what an individual considers to be good or not good. Very often an aesthetic attitude involves that instead of looking at the object (in this case listening to music) in the light of our needs and expectations, we give it enough time to reveal its own significance to us. It also means that instead of remaining confined to the outer aspects of the object, we try to get into its essential spirit. Applying concept of aesthetic attitude to Hindustani classical music, let us see how a *bandish* may be perceived. We have to attend to the *bandish* not merely because it is a composition of the *gharana* to which we belong, nor from the viewpoint of its possible salability if recorded, but for the sake of its own character and charge. Further, our attention to it has to be sympathetic as well. It will not do to merely identify the *raag* and *taal* of the *sthayi-antara* to *sam*. We have also to see if the inner details of the *bandish* are in tune and properly interlinked. This is probably the most disinterested and sympathetic way to approach form in music.

In listening to a *sthayi*, even a little wonder as to what the *antara* is going to be may weaken the requisite character of the aesthetic attitude towards the *sthayi*. But no such risk will be there if a hint about the possible form of *antara* is implicit in the terminal phrase of the *sthayi* itself because in this case, the *sthayi* will still remain the focus of our attention. It is difficult to identify aesthetic experience with mere perception, however refined it be. A music critic or musicologist may be able to perceive every detail of the sound of the ongoing music, but his experience will yet not be properly aesthetic. He does not for a while lose himself in the emotive expression of the song.

In terms of what a good performance must be, the following are some points to consider:

It is primarily a clear and correct perception of the perpetual, decorative and emotive character of all the sounds and passages that the music presents.

It is also, if not all along, the perception of the form of the *sthayi-antara* to sum and the pattern or tans. It may here be added that, in so far as the bulk of our music is set to definite rhythm cycle too, the aesthetic experience of our music is, in a way, generally bifocal. In other words, we experience not only the *raag*, but the *taal* which the music builds upon.

Finally, we must remember that, though patience is certainly necessary on the part of the *rasika* to allow the music to unfold its glories, our aesthetic experience of music cannot be said to be wholly passive. We admire the skill with which a vocalist is able to preserve the purity of the *raag* he has chosen by keeping it distinct all along from the other *raag*s which may be close to it; and we also at times anticipate, any may be correctly, the tuft of *swaras* which is to follow the one being projected presently. So, our aesthetic experience of music does not simply demand a good deal of past experience of training, but also an active and present exercise of discrimination and imagination.

In recent times, one has observed that a sizeable number of artistes prefer to do a short introductory *aalaap* followed by a *bandish*, some *aalaap* with the *taal* and the major part of the performance dedicated to *taan*s. True, the *taan*s are what often pump adrenalin into the veins of the listeners–it is the best form of showmanship. But the fact is that the *aalaap* is what evokes the true character of the *raag*. *Taan*s are a test of the artiste's skill and proficiency. *Aalaap* on the other hand, introduces the listener to the performer's artistry and creativity.

Unfortunately, most upcoming artistes tend to make short shrift of the *aalaap* and jump on to the *taan* bandwagon. It is only some seasoned performers who take you through the paces of each note of the *raag* in an uninterrupted, mellifluous flow of sounds. That is where the maturity of the artiste becomes evident. Majority of the time, especially if the performer happens to be an instrumentalist, a noisy *jugalandi* with the tabla is what takes up most of the performance. But that really isn't blissful music.

The pauses, treatment of each note and of course its combinations is what makes the melodic content of a *raag* stronger. However, pauses in music are clearly not the same as pauses or marks of punctuation in writing. The former, it is clear, relate only to the listener's imagination, not to his ear. The latter, (pauses in writing) affect the reader's understanding. Nor can we confuse pauses in music with the silence that encompasses it. The latter is merely the abiding context of music, the former, though momentary, are integral to the very form of the music as contemplated. These pauses are judged and determined aesthetically. But it would be wrong to assume that pauses in music occur only as moments of silence between the notes. A pause is also given, where the need arises, at some select individual *swaras*. The guiding consideration here is the proper and effective projection of the grammatical character and the aesthetic personality of the *raag*.

Laya is also a determinant of formal graces and effects in music. We may leave out beats or *matras* because *aalaap*, which is an important part of our music, does not employ them. But if we confine ourselves to Indian music, we find that it is material or the plurality of *swaras* is not determined by arrangement in a scale, but by the unique ordering in a melody or *raag*.

Form and *Aalaap*

Aalaap is the foundation on which a *raag* is built by the musician. It is the slow unfolding of the scale, with artistically rendered permutations and combinations. *Aalaap* of the *Dhruvapada* manner is the oldest existing and aesthetically quite important form (sub-type) of our music. Does *aalaap* have a form? If yes, it would be the meaning of form in this context. Now, as we have seen, two common meanings of the word "form" are outline and shape. In these senses of the word, it is obvious, an exposition of *aalaap* cannot be credited with form. Whatever has a shape or an outline is limited; and what is more, in most cases, it can be encompassed in attention as a distinct object with fair ease. The distinctive effect of *aalaap*, on the other hand, are those of serenity, seamless quality and an intense and enveloping, yet identifiable raagrupa. It is true that when it is consummate, *aalaap* can seem to be quite self-complete, but we may note, it appears so not in the sense of appearing rounded like a circle–for, to be sure, we do not see its outline –but in that of being wholly satisfying.

So we have to look at the other meaning of "form" to see how it may be said to be there in *aalaap*. The second sense is what we have chosen to regard as the basic aesthetic meaning of the word, that is, form as the skillful and intense inner integration of the elements of a work of art. But what are the elements of *aalaap*? The answer lies in the *swaras* to make the *raag* chosen, laya or aesthetic pace, and formal graces like *gammak, lahak, suta, meend, andolan*. But how are the elements we have distinguished inter-related? The answer is three-fold:

1. By keeping an unrelenting eye on the grammar and the aesthetic character of the *raag*, so that the prominence of the *vaadi-samvaadi* relation, as also the requisite effect–say, of devotion or valor–are duly brought out, if not at the outset.

2. Through a careful regulation of the pace of singing.

3. By means of a skillful employment of the various formal graces which enable the singer to not merely conjoin the various *swaras* but to work up such effects as those of depth and inwardness (*gammak*), twinkling accents (*dyut* and *vedanga*), up-going meander (*dagar*) and oscillation (*andolan*). The formal graces cannot be properly explained in words; they call for demonstration in terms of actual singing. If the singer tarries (or spends more time) on a *swara* with requisite tunefulness, one may "see" a line or fount of incandescence, according as the *aakaar* is slender or ample.

A leisurely (slow) passage across three or even two adjacent *swaras* often endangers the look of a concave curve. In the higher register, a return to the tonic after a steadfast (or enduring) but fine and tuneful articulation of *komal rishabh* may project yearning and tenderness, as in *Raag* Sohni's *aalaap*.

Yet all this knitting of the inner fabric of *aalaap* takes quite some time. So, considering the way *aalaap* develops, as also its final appearance as a distinct *raag* atmosphere, the form of *aalaap* may be said to be the dynamic and full-blown unfolding of a melody along determinate lines, in roughly the way in which a man's present personality is to be understood in terms of the specific talents and ideals that have determined his growth. What is more, just as the growth of the personalities of different individuals proceeds in terms of varying emphasis in different directions, and relative neglect of some other dimensions, so it is proper to suggest the identical note-by-note elaboration is not alike suited to every *raag*.

If, for instance, a sweeping descent from *dhaivat* to *rishabh* is supposed to project the quintessence of a *raag*, it would surely not be proper for the *aalaapiya* to treat the two *swaras* in leisurely isolation.

Taans

Taan is the fast and often rhythmic elaboration of a *raag's* scale. Besides the *sthayi-antara* twosome, the other important element of *Khayal gayaki* which needs to be analysed, from the viewpoint of artistic form and criticism is *taan*. As we know, this word is derived from the root "*taan*", which variously mean–to extend, spread, stretch, weave, spin out or compose. By and large, the word *taan* is taken in the light of the first three meanings listed above. It is also a kind of extension or development of the *Khayal* rendition. But what exactly does a *taan* develop? We can hardly say that it is the *raag* chosen for treatment, for, it is the clear evidence of musical practice today that what brings out or develops the nature of a *raag* is *badhat* and not *taans*, though they certainly conform to the grammatical character of the *raag* being rendered.

Conformity is one thing; development quite another. The evidence of practice rather is that *taans* are nothing but patterns that only rearrange the constituent *swaras* of the *raag* in ever more decorative ways. Be it noted that whereas the first three meanings of *taan* listed above relate specially to something physical such as a chord or a sheet of cloth, the other meanings, such as "weave" and to "compose" go well with works of art. So, one way of interpreting it is that *taan* may be taken as a composition or orderly weave which does not so much bring out the depth or dignity of a *raag* (which is essentially the function of *badhat* or *aalaap*) as the decorative possibilities within a *raag*. Even the most consummate kind of *aalaap* cannot be said to be essentially decorative though it may well be reposeful, expansive and even sublime. The decorative quality of *taan*s is perhaps the most important feature, which distinguishes the *Khayal* style from the older *Dhruvapada* form. Quite simply, the projection of *taan*s is the composition of decorative patterns in a *raag*.

In our growing appreciation of the ancient form of *Dhruvapada aalaap*, let us not underestimate the value of pure decoration in music. It is said that the ornate may be very beautiful, that in fact what is to be completely beautiful needs to be somehow rich, is a fact of experience. Decoration, by stimulating the senses, not only brings a primary satisfaction with it, independent of any that may supervene, but it furnishes an element of effect which no higher beauty can ever render unwelcome or seem inappropriate, since any higher beauty in moving the mind, must give it a certain sensuous and emotional colouring. Decoration is accordingly an independent art to be practiced for its own sake, in obedience to elementary plastic instincts. It is fundamental in design for everything structural or significant produces in the first instançe some sensuous impressions as a spot or pattern in the field of vision. But, one may wonder, is it at all proper to speak of decoration in music as an independent art? Is it not true that the more appealing *taan*s of a *khayal* singer conform to a linear pattern which can even be drawn out on paper? If yes, how does decorative music remain independent? Such questions, however, can be easily answered.

Music is not a mere juxtaposition of notes, but their ordering in respect of pitch, that is, as higher and lower. In other words, the *swaras* make a passage, a flow. But any flow, be it that of a river or of the breeze, has its own natural manner and the fact that it may be represented in a picture or as a passage in a thematic, instrumental music composition is but a subsidiary matter. The *Khayal* does not consciously follow any prefixed visual pattern used in the formal visual arts; and the conformity of his *taans* with graphic patterns is but incidental, even as a particular formation of a cloud may happen to resemble the map of a country.

We must also remember that a *khayal taan* is a mere undifferentiated flow of a particular manner, but a succession of distinct (or distinguishable) notes. What is called *daana* or the undimmed discreetness of notes and uninterrupted flow or the two essential requisites of a good *taan*, which is indeed why Ustad Bade Ghulam Ali Khan's *taans* may be said to be exemplary. In other words, the form of every *Khayal taan* is "articulate" in the sense that it is an integration of notes in which the latter always retains a measure of individuality. There is one more requirement to reach every good *taan* in the *Khayal* style of singing said to be subject. It is the norm that a *taan* should complete itself directly at the sam with split-second accuracy or a little before that point in the sthayi, where the manifestly designed approach to the sam begins.

Elaborating on the *taan* format, Dr. Anjali Mittal, in her book *Aesthetic Concepts of Hindustani Classical Music* says: "Within this overall requirements, however, it is possible and proper to distinguish the various devices which go to make the form of a *taan* and invest it with its own unique look. These may be distinguished as follows:

Segmentation: This is the device by which the wholeness of a *taan* is sub-divided into bunches of *swaras* so as to make for that appearance of inner orderliness. The segments, however, may either cover the whole *aaroha* or *avaroha* of the *raag* or a lesser number of constituent *swaras*. In the former case, the *taan* assumes the form of an up and down contour of the *raag*. It is satisfying because it is very easy to follow, provided, of course, the two overall requirements are also duly met; In the latter case, the *taan* draws the attention to and focuses it on the inner tufts of *swaras* as well, instead of letting us merely flow along the ascending and descending passages. The first kind of *taan* merely embraces and transverses the *swaras* that go to make it. The second kind projects them in a regulated way, and so, may be said to be more articulate and more deeply designed than the first one.

Accentuation: Accentuating or laying emphasis of articulations. Here, though the singleness of the *taan* may well be literally broken, it will not appear so to those who are familiar with the grammar of the *raag*.

Interspersion with formal graces: The segments of *taan*, each comprising some *swaras*, may also be conjoined by means of formal graces like suta and meend. This device not only serves to keep the *taan* undivided, but may heighten the beady appearance of the articulate parts of the *taan*.

Varying the pace or manner of flow: In so far as pace and manner are both inherent in a musical passage, the form of a *taan* can be easily made to vary by changing its tempo or manner. Some *taan*s indeed look like a leisurely meander; others seem to gallop, and some may even seem to be meteoric. What is perhaps more satisfying to the discriminating listener is variation in the way in which a *taan* may seem to flow. It may appear to be simply curvaceous, or even curvilinear or of involute segments.

Regulation of vocal volume: Aesthetically however, perhaps the most likeable *taan*s are those which invest the whole pattern with a touch of feeling and so make its form appear a little expressive by means of the subtle employment of a gentle regulation of vocal volume. The *taan*s of maestros like Ustad Abdul Karim Khan and Pundit Onkarnath Thakur and Behere Bua are cases in point. Illustrations of such *taan*s cannot however be provided in writing, for the expressiveness in question is essentially a matter of practical singing. But form in *taan*s, whatever be its specific look, cannot be dissociated from its material, that is the *swaras* it builds upon. The cramping of *aakaar* in drut *taan*s or at higher *swaras* is therefore a definite violation of the artistic form of a *taan*. It turns the latter into a mere vocal exercise and runs counter to the basic aesthetic requirement of embellishment."

Every *taan* has two aspects: one, of conception and the other of execution. A *taan* must be executed without any involuntary bedimming or obstruction of its constituent notes. But the aspect of conception demands a little careful thinking. A *taan* has to be so composed that it may fulfill the following conditions:

First, it must have determinate and identifiable relation to the rhythm cycle.

Second, it is also expected to be properly related to the *sthayi* in the sense that the way in which it ends may seem to pave the way to the specific passage which constitutes access to the *sam*.

Thirdly, in spite of being so related to both, the *theka* and the *sthayi,* it must have its own identifiable form and appear to be self-complete.

Fourthly, it should also lay due emphasis on the salient notes of the *raag*.

Some general observations of *khayal* singing, as opposed to *Dhruvapada* form would give a more expansive view of the aesthetical aspect of this music. This, in turn will sharpen what the critical perspective should be.

The form of a *Khayal*'s *sthayi* and of its numberless *taan*s arises from the incorporation of different *swaras* in such a manner that they are not only included and embraced but also at once projected in respect of their individuality. What is called the *daana* of the swara is required to be manifest all along. This is clearly not so in the case of *aalaap* of the *Dhruvapada* kind. The distinctness of the individual *swaras* as against their linkages is more clearly manifest in a *Khayal* style composition than in *aalaap*. In the case of the latter, the *swaras* are of course not absent, except when the singer tarries at a particular swara, the notes are only embraced, not projected, in an essentially flowing and undivided manner of singing. This is why, though *Dhruvapada aalaap* is admirably capable of working up the effects of seamlessness, flow and a musical atmosphere, it does not compare very favourably with the

Khayal style in respect of investing music with the suggestion of an abounding filling.

A magnificent distinctness of details is indeed a key requirement of musical form in *khayal* singing. The meaning is not merely that the *vadi* and the *samvadi swaras* have to be kept duly manifest, but that every individual *swara* has to provide to the listener something of interest. It must appear as a moment of self-repose, an accent in a flow, a step to what is to come next or a merging into or emergence from another note, in the space provided by the canvas of the *raag*.

Here, a point may be made with regard to the distinctive way in which the suggestion of space is evoked in the *Khayal* form. The *Dhruvapada* singer's *aalaap* evokes the suggestion of space as expansiveness; it seems to move on and on. In a good *vilambit Khayal-sthayi* on the other hand, space appears as roominess. Admittedly, quite a few different factors are at work here. The aesthetic pace is slow; the articulation of words is reposeful and (in principle) a little inward-looking. But the main factor which here evokes the suggestion of great singing is the intervals of silence–or the thin, leisurely and luminous lines of singing–which are made to punctuate or fall between the articulate utterance of the *bols* of the *sthayi.* However, a *sthayi* is not expected to unfold and establish itself in utter isolation. It is accompanied by a *theka* to which it is required to conform. There is room within the *theka,* as there is within a *sthayi.* Artistry could be heightened by making use of that roominess, say, when an emphasis in the *sthyai* is made to fall in the interval between two adjacent *matra.*

Finally, the *raag* form itself admits of suggestions of roominess in numberless ways. The most obvious of these ways is the inexhaustible filling of *taan*s of various kinds that every *raag* permits. Where patterning or *firat* is not quite freely possible, as perhaps in the case of *raag*s like Hindol, the suggestion of roominess can be evoked only in a limited number of ways, the more important of these being slowness of aesthetic pace or *laya,* steady articulation of individual notes and their interlinking by means of simple and flowing curves as distinguished from intricate *taans*. But we experience space not merely as something in which things are seen to be located, but also as a stretch or distance from one point to another or as an extension.

Now, the most common device for producing a suggestion of extent in music is the employment of such *taans* as it covers more than a single scale or *saptak*. What is more, if a *taan* is somewhere made to take off from a note in the *mandra saptak* and to reach up to the corresponding note in the *taar saptak*, the suggestion produced will not merely be one of a self-completing pattern, but of a pattern which seems to be considerably more extended than the space which its constituent notes take on a musical instrument. What is more, a suggestion of infinite distance can be generated through a skillful employment of but two adjacent notes. Thus, if in a Sohni rendering, after a brief utterance of the *shadaj*, the adjacent *rishabh* is projected steadily and made to fade into quiescence, the cultivated listener will get the impression that the *rishabh* is looking far and deep into the distance.

The number of *swaras* traversed by a *sthayi* can also evoke the suggestion of extent. There are some *sthayis* which traverse almost the entire musical scale. They naturally appear to be extensive than those that comprise a lesser number of notes. It is here necessary to add that extent appears in music not only as attitude, but even as depth. The suggestion of depth can easily be evoked by a *sthayi*, the *sam bol* of which is placed in the *mandra saptak*, as may easily happen in the case of *raags* like Pooriya and Malkauns. We must however hasten to add that this device of placing the *sam bol* in the *mandra* is by no means the only way of securing a suggestion of depth in music. Most of the morning *raags* are admirably capable of producing a suggestion of depth, but very few of them admit of a placing of the *sam bol* in the *mandra*.

Further, in actual life, space is experienced not merely as something that is traversed, but as something which is explored. In the region of music, this suggestion is easily evoked when two adjacent shades of the same *swara* are gently, but correctly embraced in a single flowing passage. The life-like quality of music as an art extends even further. In life, we experience time quite variously. Say, as repose and nimbleness, or as succession, simultaneity and duration. As for the first two of these, their distinct presence is clearly visible not only in *vilambit* and *drut khayal*s, but also in *taan*s of various pace. What is here important to note however, is that, in music, slowness and quickness of pace appear not merely as such, but as invested with some extra suggestions such as those of repose and contemplative quality or of gaiety and ebullience. The point is clearly seen when we reflect that running on the track, whatever be its pace, does not appear to have these qualities. In the case of music on the other hand, a slow onward movement may even come to appear reverential, for instance, a correct utterance of the *gandhar* in Darbari or the caressing descent of the phrase *Ma* to *Ga* in Lalit. It is also noteworthy that where leisurely pace appears integrated in a well-structured *sthayi*, the suggestion evoked is one of stability, in spite of the fact that movement across the various notes is actually there.

Simultaneity in music operated in three main ways: as a moment of attainment, as a process of confluence or as a background. The strains of the taanpura do not flow along with, but provide a steady vibrant background to the entire music. The *sam* is easily the most conspicuous moment of simultaneous attainment by the drummer and the singer. As a process of confluence, simultaneity is seen in the way the sarangi player tries to duplicate the patterns of the vocalist or the drummer may seek to interweave parallel patterns with the various configurations of the vocalist.

As for duration as experienced in the contemplation of music, it is not the same thing as duration measured by our watches and clocks. When, after attending a concert we look at our watches and say that the recital has taken a little more than two hours, we obviously speak of duration from the practical and not from the aesthetic point of view. Duration thus regarded, is only the length of time for which a thing lasts. In music on the other hand, duration is necessarily the material of some effect, satisfactory or unpleasant. Thus, if an important swara is not rendered long enough, we tend to quietly protest against the unsatisfactory effect. A similar reaction may take place when the musician tarries at a note a little longer than is warranted by the grammatical nature of the *raag* being rendered.

Duration in music may also work as a determinant of balance between the various elements of a recital. Thus, if the weaving of patterns (or *taans*) is done for so long that the intervening utterances of a *sthayi* are wholly ignored, the recital would come to appear ill-balanced. A similar effect may be produced if, as it is sometimes seen to happen in music of some musicians, the number of ways in which the various notes of a *raag* can be permuted is highlighted at such leisure that the flowing form of music is sacrificed for the sake of merely calculative, analytical intent. On the other hand, where due care is taken in regulating the various parts of a recital, the ending of one distinct spell of music and the beginning of another may at once be felt as a mark of adroitness on the singer's part and a welcome change in the fabric of the music itself. Thus, if a brilliant *drut khayal*, kept within limits–a sudden switchover to a leisurely *Tarana* (say in Jhaptaal)–may well strike the listener as a welcome relief, not in the sense of a riddance from something unpleasant, but as the complement of repose demanded by a burst of animated singing.

To conclude, not merely the various emotions, but many subtle details of life can be projected in music with telling effect. It is indeed difficult to think of any other art which could be said to equal music in respect of appearing lifelike, without necessarily making any explicit reference to life. Thus, as far as appreciating music is concerned, the above-mentioned observations on form, *aalaap* and *taan* need to be kept in mind. Each performance is different, but the basic framework should fit in somewhere within the parameters mentioned.

Some Modern Trends in Hindustani Music

In the last 60-odd years, there have been several changes in the form of music that one gets to hear. Political, economical and cultural developments have resulted in certain distinct changes in the music world. Critics and listeners need to hear and judge music, keeping these aspects in mind. Some of these changes are:

Changes in *raag* and *taal* presentation. Certain musicians like Amir Khan gradually compressed one *avartan* of a *taal* with the changing times. He probably realized that listeners found it a bit tedious to sit through such a slow-paced rendition. Similarly, certain *raag*s, which traditionally did not use certain notes, started incorporating them into the scale.

The duration of most performances, that is, the time spent on such *raag*s has gradually shortened. Some of the reasons for this are the long distances people have to commute to reach the recital center, problems of transportation. The number of concerts held on a Sunday has decreased, what with the television invasion.

Radio has done away with the live programmes of classical music, which had its own charm. Now the programmes are pre-recorded. Those exciting moments when the musician thought that thousands of listeners are listening to him while he was actually performing, are gone.

A great service is done by All India Radio (AIR) for building up the archival unit, both in Hindustani and Carnatic systems. Different schools and styles are represented, where forms and compositions are covered. The unit also has some rare interviews with great masters. One only wishes these were aired more often. This will raise the standard of listenership, enrich the listener in many ways and also help in preserving the tapes by using notation. Some of the studios outside the AIR arena which have mushroomed all over the country are doing monumental work by recording classical music of great value while there are others which do not mind mediocrity and hence the music churned out does little to enrich our ears. Commercialism is the key word, both for the musicians and the studio owners. The electronic media should be more discerning, if we want to keep high standards.

The audio-visual media, which is the most powerful of all the media, leaves nothing to the imagination of the viewer. The class of viewer which does not know the difference between a sitar and a taanpura, a tabla and a mridangam, at least now knows what is what. The musician who was known to him only by audio cassettes, can now see the artiste, his personality, his way of performing, emotions while presenting a *raag* and many other things. But then, is the electronic media, that is television, giving the viewer a fair chance to evaluate and understand or appreciate our music? May be not. The time allotted to classical music is far too little. The great masters of our country are presented well near midnight, when the younger generation or the tired viewer, retires for the day. It is frustrating for the musician, as well as the keen viewer and lover of classical music to be deprived of his pleasure. Concerted effort needs to be made to build up viewership of classical music. With the onslaught of cable networks, classical music has to be given predominance in programming.

As Lalit J. Rao says in her essay on *The Electronic Media and Music*, which appeared in *Vageeshwari:* "No other science has totally revolutionized man's lifestyle, his thought processes, his work and actions as the science of electronics. Today, we take so many gadgets and conveniences for granted, not realizing that in our parent's time they were unheard of. Electronics and electronic inventions have had a stunning impact in all disciplines and music is no exception. Music has been sky-rocketed with exponential speed in a short span of about sixty years into a world of sophisticated electronic gadgetry that can both be baffling and extraordinary. Electronic media advances are bound to have a profound effect on music, which is essentially a communicative medium.

The cloistered and sheltered confines of temples, churches, king's courts, small *mehfils* where the musician ruled supreme and his will was law as far as his music was concerned, where he had a devoted audience which appreciated music, have been broken down. The electronic media has catapulted the musician and his music into a bewildering world of electronic gadgetry, publicity and media hype. The musician's seclusion and anonymity have been torn to shreds and he is face to face with a multitude of people both knowledgeable and ignorant, appreciative and disdainful, his words, his music and his behaviour under constant scrutiny.

With the advent of television, the major connection between electronic media and music was radio broadcasting. Though cinema and the gramophone record preceded the television, the impact of cinema on classical music was negligible compared to that of TV. The three-minute gramophone records, however, did yeomen's service in the cause of popularizing music.

With the advent of broadcasting, music, especially classical music, was no longer the preserve of small halls and princely courts. This art form was earlier available to a select few, who either lived near the artistes and were their appreciative audience, or had the opportunity to attend and be invited to concerts held by kings, princes and *zamindars* who were often retained musicians in their courts or invited from neighbouring states.

With broadcasting, music became available all over the world. This had a very positive effect on the popularity of classical music. More people began to be aware of classical music, they could afford to listen to it in their homes, they could learn to appreciate it, understand it, become aware of its intricacies, listen to various artistes from all over the country singing various styles.

What was an unattainable object, talked about in awed and hushed tones, was brought into every home. It lost its aura of mysticism and became something available to one and all so that through repeated listening, one developed an empathy and feel for it. It became a source of relaxation, a source of entertainment, something one could turn to within the confines of one's home.

There are so many people who, over the years, have developed a very good understanding of classical music, who have learnt classical music by listening to the radio. Classical music received a great fillip due to the radio. With the advent of regular broadcasting, many musicians started performing regularly on the radio–it became a source of income for them. Along with the main performers, the insight into the functioning of electronic equipment and awareness of the intricacies of music and voice became an issue. Many a time in India the people manning these equipment were/are untrained and totally oblivious to the demands of music.

As a result, these powerful electronic media tools became a source of despair, whereas if handled by competent people, they can become a source of joy both to the musician and listener. Positioning of the microphone, balancing, equalizing, mixing, recordings, effects, are all highly specialized tasks and to get the best out of a performance, it is imperative that we learn the importance of proper maintenance and the presence of highly skilled personnel to operate these electronic instruments.

The impact recording has had on music is unparalleled. Today, sophisticated equipments with mixers, synthesizers, directional mikes, equalizers, special effects, computing techniques and what have you, have fine-tuned recording into a specialist domain.

From the humble wire recorders, gramophone and three-minute and long-playing records to the tape recorder, cassette recorder, compact disc and digital recording, we have come a very long way in sophistication and excellence in the equipment, the recording quality and the permanence of the recording.

With highly technical instruments at our disposal, the quality of the voice can be changed, special effects can be used at any stage, unwanted musical embellishments can be removed–really the finished product can be totally unrecognizable when compared to the original recording. Synthesizers can dish out any tune required, imitating any instrument desired, at the stroke of a button. The possibilities due to the advances made in this field are quite frightening at times. Each new discovery or advance brings with it a package of both good and bad and we have to accept both.

A big step forward as a result is that it has made the musician more aware of what he is performing, how he accomplishes it, what his drawbacks are. The nuances and the final points in the music may not sound as good when recorded. He is able to listen to himself as a third person and evaluate his music critically. This becomes the most important step towards bettering oneself, since many flaws get amplified through the sophisticated recording systems. The musician becomes aware of certain flaws, which he may not have known. This has had a good effect, as the musician has to be on his toes in search of excellence. He has to devote his attention not only to his music but also to all other aspects connected with his presentation time limits. Compactness, cohesiveness, voice quality, musicality of tone all through, clarity of expression; even when navigating difficult passages or flights of imagination, the quality should remain musical and in tune all the time.

Our classical music has been an oral tradition and has been handed down from guru to *shishya* by word of mouth. There are many social and musical exigencies and intricacies present in our musical system and a lot of importance is given to creating within *raag* limits. This has resulted in the development of an inadequate notation system which only gives the bare backbone of the composition. After learning a composition at the feet of the master, this notation system can serve only as a ready reckoner to refresh ones memory. It is not possible to learn a composition in the *raag* from the notation unless one has a perfect mastery over the musical system and a complete idea of the thought processes of the person who has noted the composition. With a host of recording facilities available, compositions can be recorded on tape. In addition, our music can be recorded in the form of lessons, demonstrations, archival recordings, concerts and discussions.

In the olden days, one learnt music under the *guru-shishya parampara*, which involved several years of serious study, staying with the guru, with no other diversions, with about six to eight hours devoted to the study of music and rest of the time, spent listening to others sing, others being taught, participating or listening to discussions on music. This meant a total dedication to music to the exclusion of everything else. Hence, it was possible for a student to pick up very well our complex and abstract music, the style of the guru, the embellishments, the vocal intonations, the development of the *raag* that made his master's style unique.

With social and financial pressures today, it is not possible for a student to dedicate himself totally for eight to ten years only to music (staying with the teacher has become impractical due to constraints of space and social pressures). As a result, a student learns about five to six hours a week or even may be one or two hours a week. So, how is it humanly possible for a student to absorb, learn and assimilate the rich treasure house that his guru has inherited? If he is intelligent and dedicated, he can learn about forty to fifty per cent of what his guru is willing to teach.

In such a situation, the advantages of recording are unparalleled. Compositions and discussions can be recorded during the lesson and used by the student at home to compliment his learning process. But this requires total mental reorientation on the part of both the student and the teacher. The guru should realize that he is not being taken for a ride by allowing his lessons, etc. to be recorded. Loyalty and dedication to the guru and the personal commitments that the recordings will not be misused is absolutely necessary for the *shishya*. If this sort of system has to succeed, mutual trust and conviction should be the basis of this relationship, otherwise it will remain an exercise in futility. Why not take advantage of the tremendous strides in electronics which have given us such compact portable cassette recorders and march ahead?

In the olden days ones music was considered a secret gift, not to be parted with to one and all. All this must have stemmed from a feeling of insecurity. The compositions, *raag*s were all guarded like prized possession, for fear that somebody belonging to some other *gharana* could pick them up.

With the invasion of electronic recording media, ranging

from huge recorders to micro-miniature recorders that can look like a fountain pen, or possibly smaller programmers, concerts and discussions can be recorded with or without the knowledge of the performer and the veil of secrecy and mystery that enshrouded our music has been torn to bits. Hence, attitudes will have to change completely.

Till very recently, before the advent of broadcasting and commercial recordings of classical music, it was possible to keep the different styles of music distinct as communication between places was difficult and hence, it was not very often that one could hear musicians belonging to another style or school of music. As a result, the shishya was mainly exposed to the music of his guru. Now, with radio, TV, cassettes, records and compact discs, it is impossible not to be exposed to other forms of music. Consciously or unconsciously, one is influenced by it.

One assimilates those aspects that one appreciates into ones own music. Stylistic boundaries are quickly disintegrating. Our musical milieu is in a state of tremendous flux. Old ideas, norms and teaching methods have received a stunning blow due to the impact of electronic media and it will take some time for some meaningful dialogue to emerge and grow from the rubble that it has been reduced to. Change is inevitable and one has only to take care that the change does not destroy the pristine and contemplative quality of our music but enhances these qualities and assimilates new ones by carefully choosing only the good ideas to make a composite and harmonious whole."[3]

Moving to TV and cinema, its impact on music and especially musicians has been tremendous. As far as the radio, cassettes, CDs are concerned, the musician is just a voice to the listener. At the most, there is a bio-data attached to the picture, so that the musician retains his anonymity and privacy and his communication is only through the voice. With the advent of cinema and more so television, the picture became an essential part and parcel of the telecast, along with the voice.

This throws up its own dimensions of viewers interest, in addition to listening interest, background, lighting, deportment, visual impact and cohesiveness assume paramount importance. Among many musicians, this brings about a feeling of self-consciousness instead of concentrating solely on their music. They have to pay attention to dress, mannerisms, actions while singing, and a whole host of other correlated aspects. In addition to all this, the bright lights affect the tuning of instruments. The problem with balancing, adjusting lights, rehearsals, sound adjustment, are such a tedious exercise that by the time a recording starts, the musician is bored, tired, exhausted in addition to the nervousness of appearing face to face with millions of people all over. The net result often is a concert which is a poor relation or a mere shadow of what he is capable of performing.

Classical music has very low priority on TV and hence performances by any artiste are very few–may be once in two or three years. Repeated appearances on TV may help to put the musician at ease and come to terms with the new constraints imposed by this medium; but telecasts being few and far between, each telecast builds up all the phobias and fears. No doubt these problems are faced only by those musicians who have gone from the transition of recording from radio to television. The new generation of musicians will not experience these problems as it will be what they have grown up with. A new orientation and approach on the part of both the performer and recording crew will be necessary to stop it from being an exercise in futility. This underscores the absolute necessity of highly trained crew capable of operating and maintaining the sophisticated equipment with speed; having an understanding of the music, the musician's psyche and having the capacity to put the musician at ease and thus enhance the quality of the performance.

The saying: "The pen is mightier than the sword" applies to what the print media, including books, newspapers, magazine or internet has to say. Since the time of William Caxton, when the printing press was invented, the press has played a more and more important part in communication and dissemination of information and in reality the world has figuratively shrunk.

With electronics in the print media, information gets flashed immediately all over the world. Books and magazines on music, reviews of cassettes, long-playing records bring musicians much needed publicity through the print media. Internet is the most recent invention which involves the digital transmission of coded information over telephone lines. The written or typed message at the sender's end is scanned, digitally coded and transmitted to the receiving end where it is digitally decoded and printed.

Though fast electronic printers have replaced slow mechanical ones, the time taken to send the message is directly dependent on the speed of the printer. This is the advantage e-mailing through the internet has over the fax. Now, a review of a programme in Delhi can be viewed all over the world, instead of being dependent on the more limited newspaper circulation. Needless to say, this has a tremendous impact on musicians and their audiences all over the world. The internet is also the quickest, cheapest and most effective way of disseminating information-in this case-music.

Computers have already been used in printing notations. With pattern recognition, voice recognition and mind-boggling advances in computer technology, the time does not seem far when one can sing a *bandish* in front of a computer and it will print out the notation. Learning a *bandish* will mean listening to it from a computer, with the computer correcting any mistakes. It may supervise grammatically correct presentation of *raags*. There are wonderful and frightening possibilities.

Will these advances in electronic media take over music and musicians completely? Most probably not. The soul and life of our music is human creativity, sensitivity and emotions. With the advances in electronic media, the computers may be able to churn out any type of *bandish* and *raag*; but it will have to be programmed by a human being. Therein lies the crux of the situation.

What makes one musician's depiction different from another's, apart from the mental aspect, is the emotional and creative aspect which is unique every time. It is up to us to use these media tools to our advantages, as complement to the teaching, learning and archiving methods.

Music and musicians are in a crucible with electronic media as a catalyst. What emerges from this constant state of flux, only time will tell. Change is inevitable and out age-old music must bow down to the demands of the electronic media.

It is commonly seen that as much variety as is possible by an artiste is crammed into one and a half hours of the recital. Earlier, a *Dhruvapada* recital would commence with a 45-minute *aalaap* alone. Now the sitar has replaced the veena. This is the age of *khatka, meend, gammak* and *kan* in recitals. Earlier, the purity of the *raag* was most important compared to its decorative aspect. The quest for something new is the overriding passion in music these days. On the one hand, we find a lot of Carnatic *raag* scales making their way into Hindustani classical music. Popular among them are Abhogi, Charukeshi, Basant Mukhari, Hamsadhwani, Kalawati and Kirwani. New *raag*s are being created and many of the old ones are being forgotten. In a couple of decades, some of these ancient *raag*s might become extinct.

The rendition of *aalaap* and *taan* have also undergone a change. *Madhyalaya* was the predominant *laya* earlier. Now *vilambit* and *ati vilambit layas* are more often heard. While the pace of *aalaap* has slowed down, that of *taan*s has speeded up. Vocal gymnastics and speed are the hallmark of any recital today.

One of the biggest changes in performance has been the introduction of the microphone in Hindustani classical music. Earlier, the artiste used his/her lungpower to reach the listener sitting at the end of the hall. For this, a protein-rich diet and regular exercise were mandatory. With the introduction of the microphone, musicians produce a light and melodious voice that sounds pleasing to the ear. Gone are the days of loud, strong and powerful voices. As long as it sounds good on the microphone, it is good.

In the last few decades, the names and character of *raag*s has undergone a change. Many *raag*s that were performed in the 13th and 14th centuries, have now become extinct. Nobody hears of them now.

The words of certain well-known *bandishes* have been changed over the years. They have been sung by so many different singers from their respective *gharanas* and with the passing down of the compositions from generation to generation, there have been several alterations.

A startling feature is the sudden hike in the amount of fees charged by artistes per performance. To facilitate this, organizers have to resort to sponsorship of programmers, which has further led to greater commercialization.

One positive development in the last forty years has been the introduction of music at school and college level. This has fostered greater understanding of the art form, which might further lead to a more abiding interest in it. Earlier, the only way to learn Hindustani music was to surrender oneself to a guru. The grace of learning at the feet of gurus, their reverence, which gives input to the quality of their music is certainly disappearing, for the student of today does not really think that this is important. He thinks he can become a musician with all the electronic media at his disposal and a bit of training from a teacher. But he does not know that something is lost in between. It is not just a delineation of a *raag* that a guru is teaching. It is the whole process of learning step by step, and the sanctity that goes with the seriousness of our music.

The other modern trend in music has been that today, with a degree in music, a lot of students are opting to teach it. This has become a viable means of livelihood and one of the more practical ways of preserving the art form. Earlier, the concept of a bachelors or a master's degree in music was unheard of.

REFERENCES

1. Brihaddeshi, Matang, Shloka 282.
2. *Hindustani Music*, Dr. Najma Perveen Ahmad.
3. *Aesthetic Concepts of Hindustani Classical Music*, Dr. Anjali Mittal
4. *The Electronic Media and Music*, Lalit J. Rao, Vageeshwari.

3

Music Criticism

After some details on what good music is, how it has evolved over the years and views expressed on the subject, we now come to what criticism is.

According to the Oxford Dictionary, "a critic is one who pronounces judgment on any literary or artistic work–one skilled in textual criticism." Normally, the tendency is to believe that a critic has to be critical. In other words, the critic has to be negative about a performance or any artistic piece of work. This, however, is a fallacy.

Normally, a seasoned and balanced critic gives due praise for the positive aspects of a performance and suggests measures to be taken for correcting deficiencies. This, in turn, proves helpful for the artiste and when a music lover reads the review after having witnessed the performance, he/she tends to hone his/her musical sensibility further. The other positive aspect is that organizers are also able to gauge the performance, based on a more informed perspective.

But what are the aspects of good criticism? What are the areas that need to be observed in a performance by a good critic? The following could be some of the points one needs to keep in mind.

The first aspect of any performance is presentation. In the context of a music performance, the foremost point of observation would be the artiste's personality, followed by the stage set-up. If one attends a concert of Pt. Ravi Shanker's, the sheer array of his students on the stage itself looks impressive! What follows is a different matter all together. But if you go for a fairly new artiste's concert, many times you find just a white bed sheet suffices as the platform. Many times, the stage backdrop also looks like it could do with a facelift.

Critics are usually given the front row of seats on one side of the auditorium. This certainly gives them a good view of what happens on stage but the flip side to this is that many times the speakers are parked bang in front of them. God help, if the sound balancing and volume are out of sync in such cases! Even the most mellifluous music sounds distorted to the listener then.

Two tunefulness and being in *swar* are the most apparent clauses in a music performance. If it is an instrumental performance, a critic's ears will be able to pick out any shortcomings in the tuning of the instruments. Likewise, in the case of a singer, any deviations from the notes or a badly tuned tanpura become points to be noted. A well-tuned set of instruments creates just the right ambience for a recital–both for the listener and the artiste.

A well-designed brochure, giving details about the artiste's career and a brief synopsis of a theme, if any, is an added bonus. Most often, music lovers hear an artiste for the first time in a festival featuring young, upcoming and seasoned artistes. It helps in such events if the organizers, through sponsorships, print brief introductions for these artistes. Those who are established, needless to say, need no introduction.

The opening notes of a recital, whether *Dhruvapada* or *Khayal*, are of paramount importance. It is true that a lot of artistes take time to warm up. But a true performer is one who is able to captivate his audience with the first few opening notes. Any concert of a good performer sets its magic from the word 'go.' It would be wrong to write off an artiste's performance just because he takes time to zero into the concert, but credit needs to be given to the one who has an impressive start. It gives the impression of a cohesive and well-meditated performance. What follows later may not be superb, but an impressive start collects several favourable points!

In the case of a vocalist, pronunciation and *aakaar* are things to be observed. There are singers who do not have distinct diction. Their *aakaar* is also defective. Some open their mouth too wide, while others don't. As a result, the tonal quality also changes.

Then there were those who spoke Persian and other Central Asian languages. They found it difficult to sing Hindi and Sanskrit lyrics but could sing in the Hindustani classical music scales so they invented the *Tarana*. However, there are a host of singers who sing in Hindi, but the listener doesn't manage to figure out what he or she is saying. That becomes faulty pronunciation and needs to be corrected.

On many occasions, the artiste takes time to synchronize his/her pace with that of the tabla player's. Sometimes the tabla is slow and at other times it is much too fast for the main artiste to play/sing at ease. On such occasions the main artiste often interrupts the concert for a couple of minutes during which time he/she briefs the tabla player what the rhythm ought to be. A seasoned tabla player wouldn't require this on most occasions, but someone who is inexperienced, would. As some tabla players have often said–it is a reflection of his/her capability if the main artiste has to prompt him as to which *taal* needs to be played and in what *laya.* But a concert can definitely be marred by the absence of cohesiveness between the main performer and the rest of the accompanists–be they sarangi, harmonium, tabla or tanpura players.

The beauty of a concert hinges to a great extent on *layakaari.* When the artiste comes at the right time on the *sam*, after completing an *avartan* of *aalaap*, everyone–the performer, the accompanist and the audience, experience great joy. Artistic variations of the *mukhada* before the *sam*, whether it is permutations and combinations of the *raag* scale or a simple *tihai*, go a long way in adding value to a recital. Imagine a concert where the singer/instrumentalist is perfectly tuneful, is following the grammar of the *raag*, but has no sense of rhythm. It would be a dreadful recital.

Another aspect of a sense of rhythm is that within the cycle of a particular *taal*, it is important for the critic to observe whether the artiste is mindful of each of the smaller divisions within that *avartan*. For example, if a *vilambit* in Ektaal is being performed, it is important to observe whether the words of the *bandish* are being emphasized with the *theka* in mind. Adherence to the basic pace of the *taal* creates a far greater impact on the listener than just arriving on the sum at the end of a cycle.

Too much of *layakari*, which is the normal tendency among instrumentalists of the day also detracts from the beauty of the *raag*. The initial thrill of hearing a super fast *tihai taan* as a *jugalbandi* with the tabla gives way to a certain weariness when this is repeated too often. The beauty and creativity of the notes ceases, leading to showmanship–a demonstration of the artiste's musical gymnastic velocity.

Another aspect about *laya* and music is that certain compositions lend themselves naturally to a certain tempo. For example, a *bandish* set in Teentaal can be in *vilambit, madhya* or *drut laya*. But depending on the style and compositional intricacies of the bandish, the appropriate *laya* is decided on. The intricacies of a composition get highlighted in *vilambit* and *madhyalaya*, whereas a play on rhythm and notes sparkles in *drut laya*.

The main aspect of criticism where the critic's knowledge and judgement matters, is in the area of the grammar of the *raag*. What is the correct scale of the *raag*? Which are the notes in it, which need emphasis? How is a certain note used? Is the *madhyam* used as *Dha, Pa, Ma* or *Ma, Dha, Pa*? Is the *rishabh* rendered with a touch of *gandhaar* in it or straight on? These are some questions which should arise in the mind of a good critic so that he/she can evaluate the competence of the performer. If the critic is not knowledgeable, any music should sound good or bad to him/her. However, since this is classical music, with a definite set of rules and techniques, it becomes important for the critic to gauge how far the performer can be creative within the boundaries of certain rules of the *raag*.

Sometimes the artiste emphasizes a note in the *raag*, which does not grammatically merit so much of importance. For example, in *raag* Yaman, *gandhaar* is universally considered the *vadi* or chief note. If, instead, *rishabh* is pronounced, where each *aalaap* rests on it or that the note is held for a far greater duration than *gandhaar*, the character of the *raag* changes and makes the rendition faulty. Therefore, it is essential for the critic to know the basic character of not just Yaman, but other associated and similar *raag*s. It is only with this knowledge that a critic can know whether a particular *raag* is being rendered in the true sense.

Since it is imperative to confine oneself within the boundaries of a particular *raag*, straying from the prescribed path would mean dilution of the *raag*. It also is an indication of the artiste's faulty training and inferior grasp of the *raag*. No matter how tuneful or rhythmic the artiste is, the critic, if informed, will be able to cite this as a flaw–and rightly so. It also becomes important for the critic to mention this in his/her article so that the artiste can improve his knowledge on the subject. The music lovers who attended that concert can also assess it afresh on reading about the *raag* treatment.

Another aspect of a performance which the critic needs to keenly observe, is the creation of the right mood of the *raag*. Sometimes a *raag* can have several shades of emotion in it, but a Baageshri, for instance, cannot ever have Veer Ras in it. Similarly, there are some *raag*s which naturally tend towards one of the *rasas* in Hindustani classical music. A mixture of the rasas is quite possible, depending on the mood of the artiste and the ambience prevalent at that point in time. However, each *raag* has a certain character and deviating from it radically will be incorrect. This could happen if wrong notes are emphasized on, or a particular note is prolonged unnecessarily or the very application of the notes is faulty.

There are certain *raag*s, which have a serious, meditative quality in them like Darbari Kanhada. Sohni has a certain quickness and agility in it. It is light and fast-paced. Bhairav and Todi evoke tranquility and a spiritual bent of mind. A recital, which does not comply with this basic character of the *raag*, will be considered an aberration.

Sometimes the quantum and quality of *aalaap* by an artiste is not up to the mark. Either it is too slow, making the performance boring or it is downright immature, which is what happens in the case of a young artiste's performance. The *meend*, the *murki* and the pauses between the notes all need to be rendered with a certain ease. All the phrases need to be well knit. Sometimes, a young artiste is in too much of a hurry to reach the *mukhada* and speeds up the *aalaap*. This results in an unco-ordinated presentation where the artiste immediately reflects haphazard thinking. An artistically presented *aalaap* is one which balances the weight on each note, giving a particular note due emphasis, coming again and again to rest on it using different permutations and combinations which are pleasing to the ear.

These days, the handful of critics who circulate in music circles have been somewhat lax in their approach to their jobs. There have been instances where a critic has not heard the whole concert of an artiste, but has commented on all the items presented. How is it possible for him/her to pass judgment on all the pieces of the artiste's presentation when not present physically?

There have also been instances when the same critic has supposedly attended two concerts on the same evening. The counter argument for this is that it is not necessary for a seasoned critic to hear each and every note of the concert to make an assessment. However, classical music being the evolved art it is, merits a certain amount of time–commitment –especially on the part of the critic who is getting paid for it. Critics need to arrive on time and stay for a major part of the concert, if not the whole of it. Only then can they comment on a recital.

Another aspect, which a critic ought to keep in mind, is the *gharana* (school of music) of the artiste. Sometimes the performer has trained under gurus who belong to different *gharanas*, thereby imbibing a style which blends different aspects of each. For example, Gwalior *gharana* emphasizes on– *(a)* Loud, open voice, *(b) Dhruvapada*-ang *Khayal, (c)* Straight *taans* which are normally called *sapaat taans, (d) Layakaari* in *bol-taans,* and *(e)* Use of *gammak.*

Jaipur gharana has–*(a)* Its own distinct style of voice production and application, *(b)* Short *bandishes* or compositions and, *(c) Vakra taans* and the use of small *taan* phrases.

Kirana gharana by contrast is characterized by–*(a)* The pattern of elaborating one *swar* of the *raag* scale after the other in the *aalaap,* and *(b)* An emphasis on *aalaap.*

The three above-mentioned schools of music are just some examples. Therefore, if an artiste has trained under one guru belonging to the Kirana style of music rendition and follows it up with a guru subscribing to the Jaipur gharana, his/her music is bound to reflect a bit of both styles. There are cases where the performer, over long years of riyaz and reflection might adopt a completely unique style. It is for the critic to appreciate this and not criticize, alleging that this form of music is a dilution or 'adulteration' of either the Kirana or Jaipur gharanas.

What is commonly found these days is that every musician picks up what he or she likes from any *gharana.* This is the age of radio, audiocassettes, compact discs and television programmes. Everybody has free access to these recordings and as they have the greatest recall value, it becomes easy to pick up and imbibe those aspects of a particular style that the musician likes. Gone are the days when a student spent years with a particular guru, where no other distractions and invasions were present. Classical music today is a reflection of the times and the critic needs to assess it in this new light. Looking for *gharana* purity should not be an issue. What matters is *raag* purity and creativity within its grammar.

What the Critics Have to Say

Critics of Hindustani classical music are often accused of being ignorant, biased and, to some extent, unethical. A few of them have been students of classical music at some point in their life. Others have been keen listeners, with an in-depth knowledge about the subject.

By its very nature, the genre of music review is subjective. The critic is bound to bring in his/her views on a particular performance. But the issue here is how much of a bias can creep into the writing.

There are accusations that critics can be bought over by the performer and/or organizer wining and dining them. So, a concert of indifferent standard gets written about in glowing terms while an excellent performance gets the short shrift. There have been glaring instances where a critic has ripped apart an artiste's performance in front of a gathering, followed by the same in his article. A few months down the line, you find the same critic and the same artiste–but the opinion is completely the reverse. It isn't as if there is a spectacular difference in the quality of performance. But what has transpired in the interim is that the artiste has formed a 'rapport' with the critic–getting into his good books, as they say.

This issue begs the next question: Is there a benchmark for a performance? What are the criteria for labeling a concert poor, average, good, very good or outstanding? Unfortunately or fortunately, Hindustani classical music does not provide us any parameters–at least to date. The late critic Raghava R. Menon brings home this point, in the following statement: "Unlike western classical music which has a definite structure, Hindustani classical music does not have a definition of how a Bihag, Baageshri or Yaman is exactly supposed to sound. Western classical music has notations for each stage of a composition. There are no improvisations. Therefore, it is easy to compare, say, a Beethoven composition with an artiste's rendition of the same in the 21st century, Hindustani music being innovative at each stage, becomes difficult to compare and contrast.

Moreover, the same performer may sing/play the same *raag* on different occasions and each time it will be different. At the most, as Raghava R. Menon reiterates, "one can talk about the mood of the performance. If there is a glaring shortcoming, one can point it out. But to criticize for the sake of criticizing is uncalled for. Besides, why give oneself so much importance as to sit in judgment over somebody's work?"

But the fact is that Menon had been in the business of producing music reviews for several years–and getting paid for it too. He said he does it 'for the fun of it." Probably because of this one finds that most of his pieces speak of nature and emotions rather than, say, the analysis of the treatment of a particular note in a *raag*.

Mr. Prakash Vadehra, a respected music critic and flutist, adds another dimension to the issue. He says: "If the critic is knowledgeable and well informed, what he/she writes, will always prove beneficial to the artiste. If there will be certain positive points about the performance, the artiste will try to polish those aspects further. Likewise, if the critic points out certain flaws in a performance, it is in the artiste's interest to take heed and avoid the same mistakes later on." He gave the example of the legendary Begum Akhtar. When she was at the peak of her career, she had sung a *thumri* which, according to Vadehra, had got restrained within the parameters of a particular *raag*. He mentioned this in his review and Begum Akhtar got back to him saying she would keep it in mind for her next performance.

Therefore, whether it is an upcoming artiste or a well-established one, critics feel what they say, matters–most of the time! It certainly gets the artiste some amount of publicity.

As far as accusations that critics are biased and unethical, there are several observations. It is a common thing to find critics walking in for a performance towards the fag end of a concert. But when the review appears, it is as if the whole concert has been listened to. At other times, the same critic has apparently heard two concerts on the same evening! This means he/she has been in two places at the same time, producing articles for both concerts.

The other more serious allegations are that some critics don't know very much about classical music, yet they pontificate about an artiste's work in the media. There are occasions when many of them go about asking for favours like getting conveyance to and from the concert venue. Some even ask for a recording of a performance from the organizer as they find it inconvenient to be present for it. They would much rather pass judgment on the artiste within the comfort of their own home. The review would appear. The artiste would be judged. The critic would be paid for 'services' rendered.

The Critic Reviewed

According to Nilaksha Gupta in his article *The Critic Reviewed*: "In western music, criticism is a discipline which is taken seriously. A critic there, has to be a person thoroughly trained in both the theory and practice of music. If we apply the word music criticism in this sense, to the scene in India, at least as far as pieces written on public performances of north Indian classical music are concerned, then I am afraid, we shall find there has hardly ever been any proper criticism at all. For, the nature of north Indian classical music being what it is, we shall be at a loss to find critics measuring up to western standards.

While it is theoretically possible for a critic of western classical music to acquaint himself fairly thoroughly with all major compositions and even the treatment of these by major performers and conductors, in the case of north Indian classical music this is impossible. In order the understand why this is so, we need to go into certain aspects that may sound a little too basic to the well-informed:

North Indian classical music is not written down and there is no scientific system of notation that can correctly record performances of master musicians.

There is no clear system by which a *raag* or a style of playing or singing may be judged to be correct or authentic.

In order to make value judgements that can be accepted as totally beyond dispute, one has to be a super being who has;

Had access to music and *raag*s dating back to at least the 16th century.

Knows all versions of *raag*s ever played and sung.

Knows all vocal and instrumental compositions ever created.

Knows everything about all vocal and instrumental styles, techniques and schools.

Is capable of formulating his own system for making correct value-judgements and using it impartially.

Any person measuring up to any one of these requirements is beyond human imagination.

There have been thus no music critic in the strict sense of the term in this country within living memory. So it would be better if one uses the word review in place of criticism while looking into the coverage of classical music programmes in India. For this would correctly describe the nature of the pieces that appear in newspapers. Reviewing calls for only a reasonable amount of expertise and has no academic connotations. It can be applied to all categories of writers commenting on works of literature, popular literature, fine arts and popular and commercial arts including films and TV serials.

Further, no critic of any serious art, I'm sure, would be writing in a newspaper. The greatest criticism in the history of literature and the fine arts have been published either in specialized periodicals or in the form of books.

The nature and history of north Indian classical music and the economic and social milieu of India being what it is, reviewers capable of producing pieces that describe or comment on performances of north Indian classical music in a reasonably acceptable manner, have been very few and far between. But let me, at this point clarify that my comments, whatever their worth, do not apply to music reviews written in languages written in English and to some extent Bengali, I would like to exclude the Bengali criticism from the general ambit of my piece, but, most of my observation would apply to such criticism as well, since I know that they do for a fact.

In the years after Independence and right up to the 60s, it was generally the practice of newspapers to appoint people with some kind of flare for words but a very misty comprehension of music (like a senior gentleman called Krishna Chaitanya, whose ambiguous sleeve notes decorate old LP jackets). You hardly even got to know what the music was even remotely like on the evening being reviewed in their pieces.

Classical music being some kind of a highly mystic and technical subject, nobody on the payroll of any kind of newspaper ever knew anything about such a state of affairs. This was only natural.

From the '60s, right till today, there have been only two or three people who have written with some authority about music performances. One of them is Mr. Mohan Nadkarni who has been writing for a very long time in *The Times of India* group of newspapers and Mr. Kumar Prasad Mukherjee who wrote for Kolkata *Statesman* (without a by line) once upon a time. Both these gentlemen have another sterling quality in common: they did not usually write to please any person or group of persons. Mr. Mukherjee had the additional qualification of being an amateur classical musician also.

Then later on, there was Shri Prakash Wadhera who reviewed music programmes in Delhi and at least kept his sights firmly on the music being performed and wrote with the sense of a person trained in music.

I fail to detect anybody other than these three whom I would consider to be some kind of a music reviewer of any consequence.

In the case of some others, I have some reservations: their pieces couldn't be called 100 per cent serious criticism. However, they stand out like shady palm trees in a desert of ignorance, verbiage, promotional (both self and group) exercises and sheer lack of aptitude.

This is how things stood in the limited sphere of criticism of north Indian classical music between 1960 and 1990–three reviewers of some worth to the serious listener and a whole tribe of people who somehow put a review together without meaning much....

....Towards the end of middle of the period under review, some Delhi dailies brought in reviewers who were some kind of minor performers themselves. Among these, apart from Mr. Wadhera who brought in a touch of musical significance into the reviews, the others failed to produce anything of any reasonable standard. The survival of the flowery, meaningless school, albeit with a touch of smartness, and a more modern use of the English language was embodied in the reviews written by Mr. Raghava R. Menon.

In Mumbai, P.G. Burde and Batuk Dewanji, writing in *The Times of India*, generally follow the style of Mr. Mohan Nadkarni and are doing a better job than the reviewers of Kolkata and Delhi. Readers are periodically treated to gibberish like someone's *aalaap* has been described as "close, detailed and like a needle point embroidery in Belgian lace", or, that "Bismillah Khan's shehnai is a bolt of the finest jute silk, long flowing..."

...A post-mortem of the below standard musical reviews is good in so far as it informs the music lovers that all is not well with music reviewing. For this state of affairs, the reviewers, themselves not equipped properly, have necessarily to share the major blame. But what about the large newspaper groups? Do they have any policy or priority for art and music reviews?

We live in a fairly open and permissive society. One of the easiest things to do is to become a freelancer in the art field or to masquerade as an art critic, putting the required appearances and assuming impressive pen names. They write, often play with words, and just get away, for nobody can get them for questioning and verification–indeed a very happy situation to operate in."[1]

What the Performers Have to Say

Most performers want critics to be present for their recitals. It is a different matter they often get upset if the reviewer is negative about their performance. But the fact is, a report in the newspapers/magazines and/or television, about a particular performance, draws attention and keeps the performer in circulation.

However, the well-known sarod player, Ustad Amjad Ali Khan is of the opinion that there isn't much that Indian music critics have to contribute. He feels: "let the musician do his/her work. There is no need for anyone else to be judgmental about somebody's performance–particularly in public. Ironically, it is the audience which actually decides what is good or bad, not the critic."

However, the role of the critic, especially if he/she gives a favourable review of a newcomer in the field, is immense. It not only encourages the artiste, but also gives him/her some amount of publicity. Conversely, if the upcoming artiste gets a negative review, it can cause severe damage to not just his/her ego but also future career prospects.

Shubha Mudgal, one of the foremost Hindustani vocalists to experiment with different genres of music, is of the opinion that critics must look at specific aspects of a performance instead of making meaningless comments about attire and environment. Most of the time the same adjectives like "sonorous" or "mellifluous" are bandied about. Not much is written about the application of notes, treatment of the *raag* or the kind of *aalaap* and *taan*.

Another facet of this subject is the relative 'high-profile' nature of certain artistes, in direct contrast to those who are recluse. What is often seen is the same faces doing the rounds of cocktail circuits, charity functions and such affairs. They get invited to such dos. They meet just the right people who can arrange meetings and concerts. They dress right. They talk right. What follows is that the press writes about them. Their faces get flashed on television screens. The artiste in turn gets due publicity. More concerts by him follow:

On the other hand, the hapless but immensely talented other artiste who might be residing in Surat, doesn't get seen, doesn't get written about and is thus forgotten. May be he/she makes an appearance at some government award function after a gap of a couple of years. So, the media, in its own way and circumstances in their own way, relegate this artiste into oblivion.

The point that the press can make or mar an artiste's reputation does hold some water. However, the basic ingredient of being an above-average musician is a must to make any kind of mark. Fortunately, the arts, and especially the performing arts, is one area where the government's quotas and reservations do not apply. There has to be a certain degree of competence in the individual for the audience to sit through a performance. And, without an audience there is no performer. Sitting in the confines of the home and singing or playing an instrument would be the only other alternative. So the press having a contributory role in building the image of an artiste is primarily dependant on some artistic ingredient. It is a different matter that one might be more creative or gifted than the other, but the basic requirements of tunefulness and stage presence has to be there.

Patronage: An Artiste's Point of View

Talking about patronage, Pt. Bhimsen Joshi, one of India's most eminent and popular artistes says in his article *Music Appreciation*: "The disappearance of royal patronage of classical music was unfortunate. This was an inevitable consequence of socio-economic change. Today, a large number of listeners are able to listen to very good artistes more easily than in the past. These days, the rich elite class of society has taken the place of royalty in patronizing art and culture. Their support has helped to start *sangeet sammelans* and musical concerts all over the country. Looking back, I see the fifth and sixth decades of this century as the golden period of music concerts. Effects of patronage extended by commerce and corporate sectors have not been all too satisfactory. Basically, their patronage indicates a general dearth of middle-level concerts.

How could the big commercial houses take up the sponsorship of art and culture so easily and quickly? I have seen that when a concert is backed by a big business house, the trumpet of its advertisement is quite loud and the glamour of the programme becomes an obsession for both the listeners and the critics. Worst of all, the remuneration of the celebrities performing in these programmes has increased many fold. Naturally, small institutions and musical circles find it difficult to arrange concerts of well-known artistes. We must understand that the principal motivation of corporate sponsors is advertising their product, celebrating themselves and not patronizing music as such. The main idea of these sponsors is to encourage a few renowned celebrities, whereas the upcoming and talented artistes of this generation are badly in need of a proper platform to present their music. Sponsorship thus cannot be the last word in music propagation. The truth is that unless the sponsors are music lovers, a musical atmosphere can never be built by this type of patronage.

I have already mentioned that show business, with the backing of commercial houses has entered the world of classical music. Why should the artiste be greedy enough to fall into the traps laid by business houses? Classical music is not meant to increase excitement but create mental peace. If artistes want to be showmen, the future of music is bleak. They may gain temporary and cheap popularity, but they would soon loose their position of dignity in the music world. I have always held that keeping up standards of music to the desired level is the full responsibility of the artiste. Unless an artiste cheats himself, the standard of music cannot deteriorate. If good standard of music is presented continuously, the taste pattern of the listener will be conditioned automatically. This is as far as the artiste is concerned.

Turning to the promoters, one can see that if they are musically minded and mature, things would be far better for classical music, because that would automatically improve the understanding of the artistes and enthuse the listeners to ask for good music. The congenial atmosphere for example, created in the concerts organized in Kolkata after Independence was conducive to good music and serious listening. As for the role of music critic friends, their main function should be to be constructively critical, emphasizing both strong and weak points of artistes and also in developing an atmosphere of consciousness and awareness of music among listeners."[2]

An Overview on Patronage

Music, like any of the other art forms, is a facet of society which doesn't have that great an importance as compared to food, clothing and shelter. Generally, the view is that it is a form of diversion and entertainment that people turn to when the basic necessities of life have been taken care of. Ironically, the musician doesn't think so and depends on society for his/her sustenance, which is food, shelter and clothing. So, the moot question for the musician throughout his life is should I sing for a living or should I make a living to be able to sing! It is only a handful of very fortunate musicians who can make a living out of music. Most others either give up half way in their fight for finances or try and do something else along with music to support themselves.

In terms of societal contribution, most countries rely on their governments to fund developments in art. So also is the case in India. Though the contribution for the arts might be a fraction of what it is for housing, health or agriculture, it is probably the most significant form of aid in this sphere. A large part of this fund is spent on the preservation and revival of some art forms that are either on the point of extinction or languishing because of inadequate attention. The Ministry of Culture is the apex organization which looks into the various aspects of the arts. Whether it is granting scholarships to able students, whether old masters need financial support for their livelihood, whether it is health care for artistes or whether it is organizing performances in the various cities, towns and villages of India and abroad–the Ministry of Culture monitors all this. With each annual budget presentation, funds at their disposal either get enhanced or diminish, depending on the state of the economy. Without fail though, the last priority is given to funding efforts in the arts.

The second level of government funding is provided by individual states. Whichever art form or artiste of repute resides in that particular state gets some form of government attention. It must be pointed out at this juncture that there are several art forms and artistes who continue to exist without any government patronage so far.

Perhaps we need a much more vigilant Ministry of Culture and State Sangeet Natak Akademis to fine-tune with the needs of the arts. Most of the time one notices that it is the well established art forms–in dance Bharat Natyam, Kuchipudi, Manipuri, Odissi or Kathak; in theatre, some well-known directors and a couple of traditional theatre forms, in music–a handful of Hindustani and Carnatic musicians get the maximum mileage from government patronage. The obvious reasons for this lopsided attention is the fact that most of the performers of these art forms come from well-to-do families, they can project themselves appropriately among the persons that matter, they are seen in the right places (parties, official gatherings which they get to know of much in advance) and they live in major cities of the country where accessing them is no problem. This is in contrast to the less sophisticated artiste–say a *quwalia* sitting in Indore or an octogenarian singer living in Coimbatore, who cannot, as they say, "network"

What happens is that these talented individuals lose out on the number of programmes and grants which the government doles out. Seen from a wider perspective, the term patronage of the arts then becomes quite inappropriate. Those who don't require the patronage, get it. Those who do, don't even know how to go about getting it. And most of those who have some idea about the process of getting grants/ programmes, lose out in the race to the media–savvy and government–savvy artistes who already have the means.

Apart from government-funding in music, there are certain privately-owned concerns, which have been doing work in this area. The eighties and nineties were the decades which saw the maximum enthusiasm in the traditional performing arts. All things Indian, whether it was fabric, dress styles, music and dance, were the rage. People of all age groups, who wouldn't have heard the name Gangubai Hangal, sat through two-hour concerts of these veterans. Many of them actually developed a taste for classical music during this period.

The artistes never had it so good. Prior to the eighties there was a small band of true-blue classical music lovers. They followed all the nuances of the music and they had their own likes and dislikes. But this band of music lovers in the country could not have garnered the kind of funding, high-profile audiences and media blitz which was required to make stars out of these performers. Till then most of the musicians were highly respected, but had modest living owing to the small amounts of money that they would get for a performance. As these artistes were not popular draws like what the Beatles were in the west, their performances were modest affairs, in terms of money, publicity and audience strength. The eighties brought in dramatic change. The Festivals of India abroad and Apna Utsavs within the country, which featured the cream of India's music and dance, made us fall in love with our culture. Teenagers, college kids, young adults and those in their middle age, just couldn't get enough of the performing arts. Certain cities like Kolkata and Chennai were always heavily steeped in the traditional art forms, but metropolises like Mumbai and Delhi suddenly awakened to its charms. Then there was Spic Macay (Society for the Promotion of Indian Classical Music and Dance Amongst the Youth), which took Indian music and dance to schools and colleges all over India. A lot of young children were initiated into these art forms by their parents. That became another source of livelihood for out-of-work artistes who took to tuitions.

The media also couldn't have enough of these new-born stars. Articles were written about their life histories, their tastes in clothes, food, travel and, of course, music. Reams were devoted to interviews with a handful of them. Some critical but often eulogistic reviews would appear in the papers of their many performances. Such was the time then that a music concert just had to be covered. Never mind if the person covering it did not know much about the grammar of Hindustani or Carnatic music. A lot of inaccurate statements were also made in the newspapers during this period. This was also the time when music critics were in great demand. The natural progression was, more programmes, more reviews. More reviews, more reviewers required. A few known names got identified with a particular newspaper or magazine. Realising the worth of publicity (those were the days when television had still not made heavy inroads into anything and everything) a lot of artistes in turn tried to build bridges with critics. In the process, the critic also became a figure to reckon with. He/she got regular invitations for programmes and get-togethers. Some even found their way to selection committees and audition boards. The private sector also jumped on to the classical music bandwagon because they wanted to be seen doing something socially beneficial. Apart from that, organizing such events and paying the artistes also got them certain tax benefits. Passes would be issued to the public and a full house was almost always guaranteed. A point worth noting at such a juncture is that ninety nine per cent of the concerts had entry by invitation. Only a handful of such concerts were ticketed. It stands to reason that despite being at the peek of its popularity, classical music in most cities didn't command buying a ticket of any denomination. This is in striking contrast to what it is in the theatre world where almost all shows are ticketed.

Then the disillusionment set in. Artistes would command huge fees and insist on five-star hospitality. In return, they would be unprofessional, coming hours late for concerts, throwing tantrums on stage and blaming the standard of a performance on the lack of the right "mood." Not caring much for public adulation was cited as another guiding principle in the attitudes of these artistes. Spiritualism and being reclusive were other facets which were propounded.

Unfortunately, neither the public nor those who funded these events could tolerate such lackadaisical behaviour for long. On the one hand these artistes were demanding and getting huge fees while on the other hand they were shirking their professional responsibilities by relying too heavily on artistic license. Besides, most of these performers wouldn't package their performances in the right way. The same old repertoire and long-drawn performances started making listeners restless.

Then came the age of Indipop. Youngsters identified instantly with it. The lyrics were desi, the sound was contemporary, and more important, they managed to create a lot of energy for the youth on stage. The middle aged still stayed faithful to classical music, but the crowd pullers were the Indipopers. They also got paid handsomely for their performances. They also had the edge in that most of their shows were ticketed, yet they went house-foil.

Many would argue that comparing popular culture with Classical performing arts is not fair. That is why, traditionally, all over the world the classical arts have always been supported financially and otherwise by the governments of those countries. But the sad trend in the latter part of the nineties was that the honeymoon of classical musicians vis-a-vis the youth and more important, private sponsors, was pretty much over.

People refused to buy the argument that classical music, being pure and unadulterated, required a certain mental make-up of the artiste, which could not match what was required in today's instant-coffee age. In other words, these artistes failed to package their act in front of an audience. But what the organizers say is that if you are getting paid for services rendered, you cannot but be professional. And here professional means doing a show on time, editing and conceptualizing the material for a perf0ormance keeping the audience in mind (their limited time and attention span, apart from effort and expenses in commuting distances from home to concert venue). Another factor was either their lack of understanding that striking a rapport with audiences off stage–giving autographs and being approachable should have been part of the build-up for a greater enthusiasm for classical music. Instead, most of these artistes would retire to their own domains and there would be no interaction with the public.

In other words, what started off as a wave of enthusiasm in the eighties, has ended in a whimper in the 21st century. Many people blame the classical musician for this, but time has its own story to tell.

The media, being a reflection of what the people want, also reflects this apathy towards classical music. Just a couple of newspapers carry regular reviews of concerts. Those who had regular music critics on their rolls have now done away with them. The simple logic is that if not many people are interested in listening to classical music, fewer people would be interested in reading about what happened at such a musical event. So, why waste newsprint on such a subject? What is more, the number of pages assigned to the classical arts has steadily been shrinking, making way for entertainment and lifestyle subjects. So, you might have a four-column article on Indipop artistes–Jassi's or Daler Mehndi's performance, in contrast to a short, single-column write-up on a middle-ranking classical singer's recital.

To conclude, classical music has come down the ages and will always remain with us. It is one of those rare gifts of our culture that will last forever. What will change with each past decade is the degree of appreciation for this art form.

REFERENCES

1. *Music in Journalism The Critic Reviewed Nilaksha, Rasa–The Indian Performing Arts in the Last Twenty Five Years,* Anamika Kala Sangam Research and Publications, Kolkata.

2. Music Appreciation, Pt. Bhimsen Joshi, Ras , *The Indian Performing Arts, in the Last 25 Years.*

3. Interviews with Raghava R. Menon, *Ustad Amjad Ali Khan,* Smt. Shudha Mudgal.

4

Dance and Theatre in Perspective

India has not one classical dance form but several. Each one of these has its own grammar, artistic principles and musical structure. There are some whose histories can be traced back several decades while there are a couple that got recognized as "classical" may be three or four decades ago.

There are many who learn some form of classical dance as a hobby in their childhood and youth. Very few take it up as a career though. Those for whom dance is a profession, life can be a constant struggle. Initially, it requires years of training. For most, finding the right guru itself is an ordeal. Those who are fortunate to find one, often have to juggle learning dance with their studies in school and college. There are very few parents who would agree to their children learning only dance. Equipping them with a regular college degree to fall back on in the event of dance as a career not taking off, would be their advice more likely.

Many nevertheless strive to attain a fairly proficient level of dancing despite these handicaps. Then there is the other hurdle to cross. After the training, there is the task of finding suitable platforms to present one's talent. Many times that is where dancers have a tough time. The dilemma is–there are few platforms and many dancers. So running after patrons–they could be individuals, corporate houses or the government–takes up a lot of time and effort.

If a dancer is fortunate, she gets the right opportunities. Once a programme is fixed, co-ordinating with the musicians, getting costumes stitched, making travel arrangements, all this forms part of a dancer's life.

Through all this, many of them give up dejected. For those who carry on, life is certainly not a smooth ride. Some of them just might not have the right ingredients of a good dancer. Faulty technique, deficient facial expression, bad compositions–there could be several pitfalls. Add to that the lack of time and funds to sustain regular practice. Many of them end up getting bad press.

But criticism in many cases could be beneficial for the dancer if he or she chooses to internalize the comments. But there are dancers and there are critics–and not every connection between the two is pleasant. Many times critics can be unnecessarily harsh and the dancer in the bargain may react adversely. It can be particularly difficult for a newcomer to face negative barbs from the so-called "opinion makers"

What's more, the concept of presenting the same compositions in any classical dance form can get boring and repetitive for both the artiste and the *rasika*. In fact, it is a reflection of the classical art forms that they can adapt to the changing times in an aesthetically appealing manner and yet retain their purity. Speaking on innovation in dance, well-known Bharatanatyam dancer and choreographer, Mrinalini Sarabhai said many years ago in an article entitled *Choreography*: "Today, the times are more challenging than ever. A dancer is primarily a performer with a need for communication. Most dancers are content with an acceptance of traditional patterns and do not wish to do more than perfect them, and dance them with all the beauty and virtuosity at their command. But there are others who desire intensely to discover the meaning of movement, the world of perception, the deep experience of composition. I am one of them, born with a desperate, consuming desire to create and the need to question. Almost all creative artists wish to give a larger meaning to the language with which they communicate. For this, a complete comprehension of the work is essential. To begin with the past and its meaning. Not only the technique, but the motivation behind the form ...Dance was meant to inspire, to excite, to teach man a way of life. It cannot continue to do that with old forms. Today, the dancer's message must change, though with full artistic integrity and complete knowledge and reverence of tradition. It must continue to reflect the cultural values and conflicts of our age. In India today, art has become a sedative, an indulgence, which is the surest way to kill all creative work."[1]

But in their zeal to be "creative", many dancers may develop wrong dance techniques or worse still, they might even have been taught those. Discussing faulty technique and the role that dance has, over and above the mere movement of the body, Odissi dancer Oopalee Operajita, in an article entitled *What do Dancers Create?* for the journal *Sangeet Natak* says: "Apart from the physical realities of the setting–space, light, costume, and so on–another kind of physical reality is the sheer mechanical movement deployed to actuate the dance, to bring it into being at a very basic level. But that technique does not make the dance. And in bringing this point to light, I think we are throwing the field open for a very distressing development in the contemporary Odissi. Most young (or not quite young) aspirants seem to think that getting the technique by rote makes for the dance. What they fail to recognize is that poses, however sculptured and beautiful they may be, are not the dance. And, Odissi is replete with sculpted poses, having been described as "fluid sculpture". The accent is on the word "fluid" or "dynamic" and that takes us back to the description of dance and the dynamic image: it is the transition from one pose to another, not merely the poses in themselves. Likewise, the poses themselves have meaning only in the context of movement and in a sequence. In fact, when one films a dancer and a non-dancer doing, say, the same *pallavi*, a trained eye will easily be able to differentiate one from the other. In a dancer's transitional movements there is that all-essential dynamism: in a non-dancer's, the movement is static. It is mechanical and stunted: there is an overwhelming obsession with getting the "movement right". And in trying to master the movement alone, the non-dancer loses sight of that energy emanating from within, which characterizes dance." Another absolutely crucial element of dance is music. I have always held that a dancer must know music to be a complete dancer. She need not be a professional musician, but again, a trained eye can easily discriminate between a musical dancer and an unmusical one. The latter is not mastered by music, so her movements exhibit an easily discernible lack of harmony."[2] So, if an intended dancer, the aspirant, has no musical background, and is obsessed with technique for the sake of technique, we get to see what is called the "actualities" of dance mechanical, dry and uninspired dance, visual acrobatics, without the illuminating force that comes from within. It is acrobatic, and does not provide aesthetic relish, which is what ultimately establishes *rasa*.

Then there is the other, important aspect of dance that many times can enhance or detract from the performance of a dancer. All the dance forms use *abhinaya*. Many believe it to be the soul of the dance. In her article *Abhinaya, the path to rasa,* in the 1984 edition of the *Sangeet Natak,* Sudha Regunathan says: "An integral part of classical dance in India is *abhinaya.* It does not recognize barriers of language or region, nor even of styles, call it Bharatanatya, Kathak or Odissi. It is the universal language of India, even if its currency be limited to the elite. In this respect, it is the counterpart of Sanskrit."[3]

Abhinaya literally means to "bring before the eyes as if face to face with the spectator". There are no aids such as speech, costume and bodily movement on the stage, all of which are subordinate to the most significant, viz. *sattvika* or emotional representation. This is where the eyes, the face and the hands are used not freely, but in a stylized manner, that is calculated to evoke the same feeling that attended upon the creation of the poem that is being represented. In other words, the purpose of *abhinaya* is to recreate the poem or lyric in all its intensity and subtlety. This concept is underlined in the famous dictum of Bharata on *bhava*.

Now, *bhava* may be interpreted as "causing something to be", the sense in which all the aids in *abhinaya* (sets, costume) are employed, so as to create something other than what is seen. But the finer sense of the word implies "affecting the viewer" the artiste wants for his purpose.

Sudha Regunathan continues in the same article: "A powerful device which aids the dancer in this effort is what is known as *sadharanikarana*. This can be interpreted as universalization through depersonalization. It is this removal of the elements of time, space and personal identity that turns it all into an experience that viewers can share, each according to his own light. Even though the emotion is intense and personal, it is not personalized; there is seldom a name mentioned, or if mentioned at all, it is universal, like Krishna. The outcome of all this is that anybody can share the experience; it is the *rasa* that calls for immediate cognition.

Besides, it is the aspect of universalization that keeps a *rasa* from descending into emotional outburst, even in the dancer. The moment she is swayed by the emotion she seeks to represent, stylistically, *rasa* slips away. Her purpose is or should be, at all time, to recreate before the audience a vibrant form of the lyrical poetry.

Sudha Regunathan continues in the same article: "This is where, it seems to me, dance stands apart from drama: whereas an actor's aim is to step into the role he seeks to play, the dancer does not. For, her forte is the ability to relate emotions of subtlest shades, impersonally. She is, in a sense, a lyrical narrator employing the face and hands to communicate in the language of *abhinaya*.

If the validity of the trend of this thought is recognized, it is easy to perceive what *abhinaya* is not, viz. mono-acting, which occurs when a dancer acts out different roles, switching places on the stage. It seems to me that unmindful use of narrative and apostrophic songs has led to aggravate the confusion. When a dancer employs gestures and poses to denote the numerous characters on the stage, as in a "coronation scene, or acts out the role of many princes who came to try their hand at breaking the bow of Shiva, she cannot be said to be doing *abhinaya*, whatever be the merit in such display."

We now come to the rather obvious, but nevertheless strange paradox that dance is–in terms of gender. In India, Shiva, a male God is the lord of dance. Yet, there are very few males today, who take to dance as a profession. Almost all dance forms seek Shiva's blessings before the commencement of a performance. In fact, the dancer prays on stage to him before starting his/her recital. But it is mostly women who dance. Much of it can be explained away as financial constraints–that dance doesn't pay enough for a man to support his family on it–but there are other historical reasons too. There was a time when women weren't allowed to dance. Then there were rituals which required male dancers.

In his essay, *Gender monopolies in Indian classical dance: A sociological analysis of cause and context*, V. Subramaniam makes the following observations on the subject.

"In most pre-industrial societies, dance developed as a communal activity, celebrating marriage, childbirth, harvest or a victory or warding off an affliction by evil spirits. Both males and females participated in this with allotted roles according to local custom. But as dance evolved into a more sophisticated art, with a clear distinction between the dancer and the audience, there also developed sharper differences between male and female roles and a gradual dominance of the female in dance, which came to be considered a more feminine art. In Indian classical dance, however, the evolution of male and female roles in dance was far more complex than in any other civilization. In particular, the position of the male dancer has been a paradox for centuries in south India. Lord Shiva was glorified as the king of dance from the fifth century onwards and his icon adorns the stage in present-day Bharatnatyam performances. But the majority of Bharatnatyam dancers are and have always been women. By contrast, in Kuchipudi and Kathakali (as well as Sattriya and Chhau) the dancers till recently were all men, taking both the male and female roles. These paradoxes need some explanation. It cannot be argued that either the male or the female anatomy is specially fitted for this or that dance role as both have their excellences and limitations. The reasons for gender dance relations in India are neither anatomical nor purely religious, but socio-historical."[4]

Through all these observations on dance, the role of criticism gets highlighted in its broader context. Some macro issues concerning dance and its problems have so far been discussed. But then there are specific issues concerning dance criticism and critics. There have always been debates about the worth of dance critics. Many believe they know nothing to be able to pass judgement on a dancer's work. But not all critics are ignorant and not all dancers would want to shrug off their criticism. In fact, upcoming dancers stand to gain substantially from what a dance review says or what a reportage on the programme reveals. Through these write ups, the dancer not only gets publicity and exposure, but also might get a feedback on her strengths and weaknesses (provided of course she respects the critic's perspective and has an open mind). Many times it has been seen that a dancer "agrees" when a critic has been positive about her performance and disagrees or may be disdainful when the critic is not favourably inclined. Often the line "What does he know about dance that he has written such a piece?" is heard.

Veteran critic Sunil Kothari in his article *Dance Criticism*, makes the following observations about the years he has spent reviewing dance programmes: "In the Indian context, dance criticism is a relatively recent phenomenon. In the old days the newspapers simply provided a column for dance reviews; besides this, no other space was provided in the press for dance. Most of the newspapers followed the British journalistic tradition, and in the pre-Independence era as well as the early post-Independence years, the job of reviewing dance was assigned to a music critic. This was the practice, early on, in the British newspapers, where a music critic also wrote on ballet. Till some 20 or 25 years ago, it was also the practice in India. It is only in recent years that the dance critic in India has come into his own."[5]

The scenario in the Indian context has to be seen keeping in view the nature of various dance forms, the aesthetic principles governing them, and the existing styles and schools. Dr. Kapila Vatsyayan writes in her book *Classical Indian Dance in Literature and the Arts:* "The aesthetic enjoyment of the classical Indian dance is considerably hampered today by the wide gap between the dancer and the spectator. Even the accomplished dancer, in spite of the mastery of the classical technique, may sometimes only be partially initiated in the essential qualities of the dance form and its aesthetic significance. But, in the case of the audience, only the exceptional spectator is acquainted with the language of symbols through which the artiste achieves the transformation into the realm of art. The majority are somewhat baffled by a presentation which is obviously contextual and exclusive, but which derives from the traditions to which they have no access. Although they are aware that the dance is an invitation, through its musical rhythms, to the world in time and, through its sculpturesque poses to the world in space, in which the character portrayed is living, they are unable to identify themselves with him. Far less are they able to attain such identity with the dancer in his portrayal of the particular role."

This being the state of affairs–which as partially changed in account of several strategies employed by dancers and with dance–appreciation courses, lec-dems, etc.–readers of reviews who have not seen the performance at best get only an impression of the event. Dr. Sunil Kotari continues in the same article: "Reviewing dance, on the other hand, makes several demands on the critic. He is expected to be well-versed in the technique of dance and music, the aesthetic theories governing dance, as well as the property, theme and content of a particular performance. This is a tall order, but only one who has some knowledge of these matters is really qualified to review dance. Since the thematic content of our classical dance derives from the epics–the *Mahahbharata* and *Ramayana*–and other mythological lore, knowledge of this genre of literature is a must. So far as the older generation of critics is concerned, their acquaintance with this literature is fairly sound. There are several versions of mythological stories in different parts of India and the interpretations of dancers are likely to differ. In this situation, familiarity with mythological literature helps a great deal.

Knowledge of Sanskrit is necessary for the dance critic in India. The manuals dealing with the technique of Indian classical dance are in Sanskrit and so are the commentaries on these manuals and rhetorical works. The *Natya Shastra*–dealing with dance, drama and music–is among the important texts in the field. The study of these texts helps one acquire a sound knowledge of the aesthetic principles of Indian dance as well as its technique. However, one cannot understand dance technique only by reading these manuals. What helps a dance critic most is practical knowledge of dance; the technical knowledge gives his writing a sharper focus and insight.

There is another difficulty ahead for the critic. Although, in the Indian context, a critic is expected to review different dance forms–Bharatanatyam, Kathak, Manipuri, Kathakali, Kuchipudi, Odissi, Mohiniattam, etc.–it is almost impossible for him to know all the languages in which the songs in these dances–to which the *abhinaya* is done–are rendered. However, there is at times almost a one-to-one correspondence between the word sung and danced through *angikabhinaya*–including the *mukhajabhinaya* and the *hastas*. With knowledge of the *hastas* used to tell a story, it is possible for a critic to understand the import of the songs.

Whereas a dancer can learn dance at various institutions, a dance critic in India has to be an autodidact. The only way he can learn his trade is to watch dance continuously. There are no facilities or evolved methodologies of learning dance criticism. Even at the few Indian universities where dance departments exist, I do not know of any course for dance criticism introduced so far. It would help if such courses were introduced in the dance curricula. The discipline of dance criticism could then develop in this country and could play an important role in the development of dance.

The existing body of dance criticism is meager. As

mentioned earlier, the subject has received attention only in the past two decades (now close to three).

No systematic study of the history of dance criticism in India has been undertaken so far. In the early '50s, the role played by Dr. Charles Fabri in Delhi to enthuse people to watch dance was significant. With the formation of Sangeet Natak Akademi in Delhi and its counterparts in the States in the '50s –as well as other government and private agencies promoting dance–public interest in dance and reporting of dance events in the press received a fillip. But it is only with the boom in magazines and newspapers with art pages, offering more space than was earlier available for dance reviews–that the role of a dance critic has assumed some significance.

There is little critical writing on dance that the critic can fall back upon. The available books on dance are of diverse nature–ranging from scholarly works to popular writings. There are few research journals publishing papers on dance. There is no periodical devoted exclusively to dance such as *Dance Magazine* in the United States and similar publications elsewhere in the West. The only Indian periodical comparable to *Dance Magazine* is *Sruti* published from Madras, which covers both classical music and dance (with an emphasis on Carnatic music and the dance tradition of South India). Here, classical dance is discussed in detail, and the criticism is both informed and technical.

No organization for dance criticism has yet been formed in India. There is no forum where critics can offer their opinions for debate and counter-criticism and work towards a definition of their discipline, creating standards and exchanging ideas. Archives (like the Dance Museum in Stockholm and the New York Public Library) and museums would help the development of dance criticism. Access to archival material is essential for serious study of dance."[6]

Obviously Mr. Kothari is referring to the early '90s, when classical music and dance was being given a lot of attention when he makes the following comments. "In recent times, we have seen a proliferation of newspapers and magazines where dance is given a good deal of space. There are regular dance reviews in the newspapers, weekly columns in the magazines, curtain-raisers on the eve of major dance events, as well as frequent interviews with dancers. Since the available columns have to be filled, knowledgeable dance critics today are much in demand! Well-equipped critics have an important role in this situation–critics who possess a sophisticated and technical understanding of dance; who can anticipate significant changes in dance induced by dancers and choreographers; who can recognize how these changes are related, and the influence they have on the other arts; who can develop a language and critical terminology to record, analyze and share their insights. Such critics can indeed contribute to the development of dance in India...Dance criticism cannot remain limited to reviewing pure and simple; it much act as a vehicle of change and mould public taste accordingly." However, now in 2004, the dance scenario is not the same.

For the last one and a half decade, apart from writings on dance in newspapers and magazines, there is television coverage too. It is unfortunate though, that along with shrinking space in the print medium, television too treats classical dance as a step child. It is often left to Doordarshan to showcase some of the dance performances. It is indeed sad to see a great performer of Kathak, Manipuri, Odissi or Bharatnatyam fighting for the spotlight with a semi-clad, 18-year-old model. But that's how we appreciate dance today. There aren't too many takers for it in India.

But the good thing is that it is gradually increasing in popularity abroad. Speak to any Indian Council for Cultural Relations (ICCR) officer and they will tell you they receive the maximum requests for dance recitals from India. Perhaps the colourful costumes, grace and intricate movements are an eyeful for them while back home in India.

It is time we took a fresh look at our classical forms and injected some dynamism into them. Traditions need to continue, but they also need to take into account the changing trends of the modern world.

Theatre Criticism

Theatre in India, like anywhere in the world, has always survived despite the many hindrances it faces towards its sustainability. Thanks to those who retain the fire in their bellies to make social comments, in India, theatre still has a following, even though the numbers are not large. There are different kinds of theatre though, that co-exist in India–the folk or traditional theater, the so-called upper class English theatre and the acts put up by students from theatre schools. But theatre, whichever "type" it may be–has constraints of not just finances, but also of getting together for rehearsals, not one person, but a whole production team together, at the same place, at the same time, every day. It could be a daunting task, but it works when the entire team of people is equally motivated. Then there is the other big hurdle of sponsorships. Very few theatre productions get sponsorships, whether private or public. When the government tries to lend a helping hand, the quantum of funds doled out is so meager that the luxury of putting together a well-rehearsed, well-thought-out play is difficult to come by.

But with the changing times, theatre has adapted various means to show a mirror to the world. One of those has been to use the stage, rather than to circulate among the audience. Speaking about his personal preferences between the *anganmanch* and open-air productions, noted theatre director, Badal Sircar said in his Sri Ram Memorial Lecture IV: "I personally feel more at home at the *anganmanch*. I believe there is still a lot to be explored there because it gives something in terms of intensity of communication, which I cannot have in open air. At the same time, open-air performances allow us to go where the people are and that almost always over-compensates what we get in the *anganmanch* productions."

India's traditional or folk theatre normally has open-air productions and it has been considered the basis for all other theatre movements in the country. However, noted theatreperson Nemi Chaṇdra Jain, in his article *The Use of Tradition in Theatre* written way back in 1984 recalls: "I am reminded of a seminar on playwriting and play production about 24 years ago. When in one of its sessions, it was suggested that modern Indian playwrights and directors had something to learn from what was then called folk theatre, a number of participants ridiculed the idea or were cold and skeptical. They indignantly asserted that folk theatre might be alright for the villages, but modern urban theatre originating from Western inspiration could grow only along western lines. Naturally, the very few protagonists of traditional theatre present there were regarded as obscurantist intruders.

Today, the wheel seems to have turned full circle.

After more than a century of almost barren attempts at playwriting and staging after western models, our theatre seems at last ready to reject this imitative pursuit and to venture into its own distinctive, indigenous territory. Many factors are responsible for this development: impact of the widespread quest for an Indian identity in all aspects of life in our country, including the arts, particularly the theatre; a growing awareness of and dissatisfaction of the imitative nature of our past dramatic efforts and the desire to go to our own roots; increasing exposure to our own traditional theatre forms and their amazing vitality, aesthetic freshness and popularity with people; worldwide disillusionment with realistic theatre and the search for alternatives; influence of the plays and performances.

Thus, the contours of a fresh, innovative and flexible dramatic form have gradually emerged, enabling the playwright to telescope different points in time and space, to bring in many levels of reality simultaneously, or to negotiate them freely in any order. The new form promises to restore the essential imaginative, poetic character of drama suitable for presenting complex human experience.

Another important result of this change is that this theatre idiom transcends regional, linguistic barriers without loosing its rootedness and distinct local flavour. For the first time after almost a 1000 years, an Indian theatrical form seems to be emerging.

Along with some spectacular successes, the work in the new idiom has also highlighted a number of problems inherent in such an effort. Our tradition is so long and varied, that without some social and artistic vision, without a minimum intellectual and aesthetic equipment, it is impossible to select from it what is living and aesthetically relevant, and to reject what is decadent and obscurantist. It cannot be asserted that the work done so far has always given evidence of such awareness.

Traditional theatre survives only in the countryside from which most of our west-oriented urban theatre people have remained cut off. There is a real danger, therefore, that like many westerners, they may also be attracted towards the "exotic" in the traditional theatre forms, mostly for their novelty and appeal, for the fashionable city crowds, rather than for the artistic relevance of these forms.

Experience so far has revealed that results are good when the play is strong and well-constructed, or when the theme is based on myth, legend, folk-tale or some ritualistic episode; and when the director and performers have had prolonged and deep association, experience and exposure to traditional theatre, especially its elements like music and dance."[7]

But prolonged exposure to various forms, and prolonged periods of refining a theatre production requires money. And that is scarce to find in a country like India, more so, since it is to do with the arts–a subject that isn't as important to the nation as food, shelter and health. In the following excerpt from his article entitled *The Economics of Good Theatre* in the book *Rasa*, Rudraprasad Sengupta throws light on just how much the Indian government helps theatre: "In India, the Sangeet Natak Akademi, founded in 1953, offers grants to various performing arts organizations covering music, dance and drama, promotes research organizes seminars and festivals, and subsidises publications. Its pitiful subventions to theatre troupes have been Rs. 1,44,980, Rs. 1,76,500 and Rs. 1,74,500 in the years 1962-63, 1972-73 and 1979-80 respectively. Its budget for 1988-89 was a meager Rs. 1,200,000

(Compare this to the $1,75,000,000 budget of the National Endowment for the Arts in capitalist USA, where the strident critics of the poor governmental funding for artistes cannot even begin to realize how fortunate their situation is in comparison to India!)."[8]

Though most theatre groups find it difficult to make ends meet, those in English theatre seem to have found some ways to skirt the issue. Their plays run to packed houses, with tickets priced much higher than the vernacular language theatre. In the late '80s and early '90s, the trend of supper theatre caught on in some of the metropolises. Audiences had to pay steep ticket charges to watch the play and partake of a five-star meal subsequently. Needless to say, these events primarily had venues in five-star hotels. Despite all the marketing hype, unfortunately, English theatre was often dismissed as non-serious by those who have been considered knowledgeable in the field. Most of these productions have been accused of titillation, with the emphasis on sex and double entendres. Some even consider them to be "foreign" and not part of Indian culture.

Discussing this very perspective, Ananda Lal, in his essay *Some post-colonial hopes* in the compendium *Rasa,* says: "English-language theatre in India has traditionally regarded by critics as a cul-de-sac. Barring some interesting amateur experiments by a handful of groups in our four or five megapolises, nearly 50 years of using English as the essential link language in an independent nation, has not produced significant results on stage. This state of affairs may encourage people to argue that it proves empirically that the language itself is antithetical to the native creativity of Indians. That this is patently untrue is established by the fact that literature written in English by Indians–notably poetry and novels– has flourished in the same span of time to the extent that many recent Indian–English works of fiction have won or been nominated for international literary awards. It may be worth speculating why drama has remained an under-developed genre in such a context.

Of course, this whole subject is a non-issue to a weighty

percentage of Indian intelligentsia who asks what justification there can be to support or even have theatre in an alien tongue. (They seem unaware of the contradiction that much of their debate is conducted in English in any way, specially when intellectuals and academics from different regions fight it out at national seminars or conferences). The charge that English is alien is itself open to logical questioning. Presumably, the alikeness arises from its geographic origins in a different land and its historical imposition upon our countrymen by colonial rulers. But by those tokens Urdu must be alien too, descended partly from the Persian imposed by our Muslim Sultans and Shahs before the British. The only difference is time. These languages gradually naturalized themselves, just as English has done in 200 years, with the result that many turns of phrase in Indian English are unintelligible to non-Indians.

There are certain factors that are responsible for the malaise that affects English theatre in India. The foremost is that it has become associated with light entertainment. Quantitatively, English language productions in India have increased manifold over the output in the 1960s and 1970s. Most of these originate in Mumbay, where the recent rise in viability of English theatre can be directly related to a steadily growing clientele of playgoers whose main interest, however, appears to be cheap thrills of both visual and verbal varieties. Despite the encouraging trend of more and more scripts being written in the Indian-English actually spoken by ordinary Indians on the street, their content moves between sex comedies starring heroines in scrapes, necessitating various stages of disrobement and ostensible satires comprising skits laced with dubious, if not outright obscene, double entendres. Mumbay producers have abdicated their responsibility to provide socially conscious English theatre, choosing the soft option of farce and cheesecake, which keeps their cash registers ringing all over the country."[9]

In any case, there is a paucity of plays written in English by Indians. The stage cannot subsist forever, nor can it grow on a diet of foreign drama, whether originally in English, translated into English, or adapted to Indian conditions. This is the other reason why Mumbay theatre, although so thoroughly professional in every way, still cannot make a permanent contribution. In theatre history, significant movements have always occurred in conjunction with original playwriting–nobody apart from literary comparists remember a period for its translations, adaptations or revivals. We require many more playwrights to compose serious drama in English so that a body of dramatic texts forms, that can sustain productions in English.

However, theatre is not just about language. It is a performing art that includes all other performing arts too–whether it is dance, music or, these days, even the audio-visual. Talking about the role that dance in theatre plays, Dr. Sunil Kothari says in an article entitled *Dance in Theatre*: "What Bharata conceived of, *natya* with dance as its integral element, is perhaps no longer possible in today's theatre. No genius like Rabindranath Tagore is poised to storm the artistic world with innovative *nritya-natya* like the ones he composed. Neither is it essential to fall back upon dance unless the director wishes to employ it as an artistic need. Those who, in their mistaken enthusiasm, use dance and music to link the traditional with the modern theatre, have not understood its purpose. They have generally failed as their attempts appear as a mere imitation of successful directors. In such cases, the issue of "invented tradition" appears to be operating. The traditions of dance are not living traditions in all parts of India and where they do not form part of the regional cultural expressions, it is not necessary to use dance to build up linkages with the roots. Such attempts are divorced from ground reality and consequently look superimposed. Still, an acquaintance with classical, traditional and folk dances always helps theatre actors and directors. But if dance is not used as an inevitable way of expressing emotions with sensitivity and propriety, it loses its relevance in theatre. Dance has a special kinetic language with a complex vocabulary of *mudras* which are a part of our classical forms. Since India boasts of a rich dance heritage, the challenges it poses to theatre are inevitable and, as noticed in a few instances, have recently met with happy results."[10]

That was the critic's perspective. But if one were to look at the role of music in modern theatre, it can be said that though it may not stand out in terms of path-breaking innovation, yet music has now become so important and integral to the performance that it has acquired the status of a theatre language like that of the dramatic text itself. It has its own channel of communication. From the *Natyashastra* to the other treatises, all have laid great emphasis on music in drama. In all traditional forms, music and movements are integral to the performance.

The primary concern of theatre as a public art is communication, which is opened with the active involvement of spectators with theatre. Theatre music greatly helps in opening the channels and smoothens the flow of communication. In the new theatre, music also helps the spectators in providing multiple perceptions of the performance.

Perfectly co-ordinating all these facets of theatre, be they music, dance, scriptwriting or dialogue delivery, requires time and effort. However, there is no set method to get it right. In fact, the number of workshops on theatre training are on the rise and each follows its own style. Commenting on this, Suresh Awasthi writes in his book *Performance Tradition in India*: "While in other performing arts–music and dance–there are age-old traditional systems of training which we expect a musician or a dancer to go through, formal training for a modern actor was not given much priority. Ours is a performance tradition in which a performer has always received training often within the family and through the process of imitation and inheritance. In several forms of theatre and dance, there is a strong input from martial art also towards training a performer. For instance, Kathakali has evolved a sound system of training with several exercises and movements taken over from Kalari, the martial art of the region, including its massage system to make the body supple.

With the breakaway from the naturalistic spoken theatre in the early '60s, several directors of the new theatre used yoga, martial arts, circus skills, gymnastics and acrobatics to impart physicality and plasticity to a theatrical performance and evolved their own system of training. These systems are primarily suited to their own production, but also have wider applicability.

Training exercises of marital arts, though developed for their carry-over-value in combat, have the inherent quality to help the actor develop stamina, reflex action and performing ability. A whole range of exercises of all the marital arts greatly help the performer in exploring the space and in developing a strong and intuitive sense of the dynamics of the body.

Training through marital art also helps harmonization of physical and psychological impulses and cultivates a sense of rhythm. In fact, these days, training and preparation for the performer has acquired such an importance that for the directors of the new theatre, actors' training and preparatory workshops have become more important than the conventional rehearsals."[11]

The training and preparation for the performer has acquired such an importance that for the directors of the new theatre, actors' training and preparatory workshops have become more important than the conventional rehearsals."

But despite certain limitations, whether it is in the area of training, language or music, Indian theatre has been able to generate enough talent and has tried, through varied artistic expressions, to portray what the society is. Theatre has, by and large, done a good job of showing us where we stand, our biases, our weakness and our idiosyncrasies. Unfortunately, many of our truly talented actors, directors and scriptwriters have turned either to television or to films, the reasons primarily being financial and, of course, a larger audience. But when it comes to true artistic expression, most of them still keep coming back to theatre periodically.

REFERENCES

1. Choreography, Mrinalini Sarabhai, Sangeet Natak Journal, Sangeet Natak Akademy (SNA).
2. *What Do Dancers' Create?* Oopalce Operajita, Sangeet Natak Journal, S.N.A.
3. *Abhinaya, the Path to Rasa,* Sudha Raghunathan, Sangeet Natak, SNA.
4. *Gender Monopolies in Indian Classical Dance: A Sociological Analyses of Cause and Context,* V. Subramaniam, Sangeet Natak, SNA.
5. *Dance Criticism,* Sunil Kothari, Sangeet Natak, SNA.
6. *Classical Indian Dance in Literature and the Arts,* Dr. Kapila Vatsyayan.
7. *Use of Tradition in Theatre,* Nemi Chandra Jain, Sangeet Natak, SNA.
8. The Economics of Good Theatre, Rudraprasad Sengupta, *Rasa–The Indian Performing Arts in the Last 25 Years,* published by Anamika Kala Sangam Research and Publications, Kolkata.
9. Some post-colonial hopes, Ananda Lal, *Rasa–The Indian Performing Arts in the Last 25 Years,* Published by Anamika Kala Sangam Research and Publications, Kolkata.
10. *Dance in Theatre,* Dr. Sunil Kothari, Sangeet Natak, SNA.
11. *Performance Tradition in India,* Dr. Suresh Awasthi.

Conclusion

Our performing arts, particularly Hindustani classical music, have always generated a certain amount of awe among most people. Many of them don't really understand its intricacies and technicalities. But the general perception among the uninitiated is that it is being presented after years of practice and contemplation–that it is, in many ways, esoteric.

So informed criticism, which looks at both the positive and the negative aspect of the Indian classical arts is a great help both for the audience and the artiste. Criticism from the press, whether print or audio-visual, is one aspect. But perhaps criticism and appreciation from those within the field, whether they be musicologists, dance scholars, experienced theatre persons, cultural commentators or artistes themselves is equally important.

Those who work in the arts are probably better equipped to talk about the operational difficulties and shortcomings. It is their years of experience which can give that perspective. That is why it is useful to have seminars on a regular basis, where professionals in that particular field of art come together and throw light on what are the deficiencies and also record the developments that have taken place.

Based on these discussions, the government, whether in the State or at the Centre, can take action to improve situations. It is true, of course, that a lot of seminars are held and heated discussions take place. But nothing much follows after that– people just go back to their own worlds and there is no concrete development. What remains after these discussions is reams and reams of transcribed material that is left to gather dust in some library.

Criticism, nevertheless is necessary. For an artiste, especially an upcoming one, any kind of criticism is a helpful suggestion for improvement. But malicious criticism can be devastating for the morale of an artiste.

Critics in newspapers and magazines are notorious for their ignorance of the subject they are reviewing. Many of them say something just to show their adeptness at a turn of phrase. But that may not go down well with the artiste. It might be a careless comment on the part of the critic, but for the artiste, it could lead to a serious reworking of earlier training.

Most established artistes, however, don't pay much heed to what critics say. In fact, the general perception is that any negative comment made by a journalist is brushed aside with the remark: "What does he/she know about the subject? Has he/she learnt the form?" But that same artiste feels pleased when a coverage by the same writer is positive. The artiste immediately "agrees" with the comments. What works, therefore, is positive publicity. Artistes, howsoever well-known they may be, would generally not dislike any favourable comments from the press.

Criticism also makes the audience more informed. Many of them may want to verify whether what they thought of a performance is echoed by someone who might "know". Sometimes what appears aesthetic, might not be correct technically according to that particular art form. These are things that an attentive audience can pick up from an informed critic. In the long run, this helps in nurturing a mature audience.

Another merit of criticism is that organizers of cultural programmes who might not have attended a particular artiste's recital or a particular troupe's concert, may read about it or hear from other informed persons about it and that's how word gets around. This, in a way, keeps artistes, organisers and programmes going.

Many times it is the same set of performers one gets to see. That might not be a healthy practice–what tends to happen then is that those artistes become in some way indispensable, commanding high remunerations, while those who are struggling to get recognition, never find a suitable platform.

Thus, criticism can play an important role in the betterment of the performing arts by showcasing new talent, projecting their cause and giving the audience a wider choice.

Bibliography

Aesthetic Concepts of Hindustani Classical Music, Dr. Anjali Mittal, Published by D.K. Print World, New Delhi.

Dance Dialects of India, Ragini Devi, Motilal Banarsidass Publishers, Delhi.

Enlightening the Listener, Contemporary North Indian Classical Vocal Music Performance, Dr. Prabha Atre, Munshiram Manoharlal Publishers, New Delhi.

Excerpts and quotes from several issues of *Sangeet Natak*, the Sangeet Natak Akademi Journal, New Delhi.

Hindustani Music, Dr. Najma Parveen Ahmad, Manohar Publications, New Delhi.

Interviews with Ustad Amjad Ali Khan, Smt. Shubha Mudgal, Pt. Deepak Chatterjee and the late Shri Raghava R. Menon.

Invitation to Indian Music, Sakuntala Narasimhan, Arnold-Heinemann Publishers, New Delhi.

Rasa–The Indian Performing Arts in the last Twenty-five Years, Editors: Bimal Mukherjee–Music, Dr. Sunil Kothari–Dance, Dr. Ananda Lal–Theatre and Dr. Pabitra Sarkar, Chairman, Editorial Board, Anamika Kala Sangam Research and Publications, Kolkata.

The Electronic Media and Music, Lalit J. Rao, *Vageeshwari,* Department of Music, Delhi University, Delhi.

The Life of Music in North India (The Organization of an Artistic Tradition), Daniel M. Neuman.

Studies in the Natyasastra, with Special Reference to the Sanskrit Drama in Performance, G.H. Tarlekar, Motilal Banarsidass Publishers, Delhi.

Index